Kibbee 'n Spice and Everything Nice

First Paperback Edition 1999
Copyright © 1999 by Janet Kalush
Published in the United States by J. Lorraine Co.
6346 Lake Drive, Haslett, Michigan 48840
Tel: 517-719-3919
JLorraineCo@aol.com
ethnic-cookbook.com
fax:517-339-4007

ISBN 0-9672663-0-0

Library of Congress Catalog Card Number 99-64051

Printed in the United States of America

Third Printing

Photography by Lights On Studio, Lansing, Michigan
Edited by Elizabeth Johnston, Okemos, Michigan
Cover designed by Barbara J. Gunia, bj Graphics, Ypsilanti, Michigan, gunia@aol.com
Book designed by Jeff Fillion, Jeff Fillion Design, Lansing, Michigan, jeff@fillion.com
Printed and bound by Sheridan Books, Chelsea, Michigan

Contents

(Arabic recipe title shown in parentheses)

Disclaimer about nutritional values

The nutritional values shown with the recipes in this book are approximate only and are shown strictly for comparison. Because nutrient values will vary according to the product brand, quantity, and type of ingredient used, neither the author nor the publisher represents these values to reflect the exact nutritional content of these recipes. Individuals needing specific nutrient values should compute the values themselves.

Foreword

Janet Kalush and I are both of Lebanese heritage and are both lovers of Lebanese food. While examining the recipes of Kibbee 'n Spice and Everything Nice my ample Semitic nose went on a journey of wonderful aromas and tastes from my childhood. I grew up in Toledo, Ohio. My parents were both 100% Lebanese, and my mother was a 100% great Lebanese cook. Although my parents lived on a meager weekly salary earned by my father as a meat cutter and my mother as a seamstress, we ate like royalty.

On Sundays after church, dinner at our home was the highlight of the week. All our relatives—uncles, aunts, cousins, and Sittee (Grandmother) and Jidou (Grandfather), if they were in town—would wind up at our house for drinks, mezza, and an unbelievable feast. The beginning was hummus with tahini, baba ghanoug, lift, olives, gibnee, sliced tomatoes, sliced cucumbers, and lots of syrian (pita) bread.

There were soft drinks for the children and arak and whiskey for the adults. Then came the main course . . . raw kibbee AND baked kibbee, koosa, djaj ma limoon, roz b shiriah, imjaddrah, lubee ah laham, warek eenab, hashwa, yabrak malfoof, sheigh il mihshee, and plenty of salata . . . and of course laban. I'll let you look up the English translations so you'll be overwhelmed at the variety and quantity of our Sunday meal. And we had leftovers even after sending care packages home with some of the relatives.

My, oh my, how I remember that bouquet from my childhood . . . the smell of garlic, olive oil, lemon, mint, zata . . . .. And my, oh my, how I remember the sights of those mouth-watering dishes—the sign of the cross in the middle of a plate of raw kibbee, the steam coming from the lubee and rice, and from the grapeleaf and cabbage rolls . . . the story telling and laughter from all who gathered. It was a blessed event on a blessed day.

I hope Janet's cookbook will take you on a similar journey of great memories and delicious food.

Allah Mah Uck. (God be with you)

Jamie Farr
Television and movie actor

Village of Deir Mimas, circa 1971

A Little Bit of Lebanon

This part of the Middle East was known in the Bible as the land of milk and honey. The Phoenicians settled on the coastal lowlands of Lebanon about 3000 B.C. and established one of the most influential cultures of the region. By around 1200 B.C. they had become a strong sea-faring nation and went forth into the Mediterranean to spread their culture and goods.

During this time the alphabet came into use to aid international commerce. It remains a question as to whether the Phoenicians invented the alphabet or adopted the concept from an earlier source. Until that time, writing consisted of pictograms, which involved hundreds of different symbols. Today the official language of Lebanon is Arabic, but English and French are widely spoken.

In 1926, Greater Lebanon was renamed the Lebanese Republic, and in 1946 it gained independence. Between 1975 and 1991, a devastating armed conflict left the country in a ruinous state. This conflict was described by the president, reflecting the opinion of most Lebanese, as "the war of others on our land." The reconstruction of Lebanon began in 1994, and the country is now on its way to economic recovery.

Lebanon is one of the world's smallest countries. It is a very narrow coastal strip with several major cities. The area has cool, rainy winters and hot Mediterranean summers, while the spring and autumn are warm and dry. A mountain range creates breezes that make the summer comfortable. Lebanon averages 300 days of sunshine per year. In some spring months, one can ski in the mountains and swim on the coast on the same day. In the mountains there is heavy snowfall from December to May.

Of all the Middle Eastern countries, Lebanon is the most densely wooded. There are three or four species of the famous cedars of Lebanon. Lebanon's great forests, mentioned in the Old Testament, once covered most of the country.

Camel caravans have given way to modern transport, but in the Bekka Valley there are camel rides for tourists.

The *dubka* is a folk dance performed all over the country. The traditional costume is from the mountains, and the dance portrays all aspects of village life. Belly dancing is also popular, and its origins are lost in history. Professional belly dancers can earn large sums for a single performance. Others, who volunteer to belly dance at special occasions, make do with contributions from the audience. Etiquette requires that you tuck rolled or folded bills into the bra or waistband of the dancers without too much physical contact. The music for belly dancing consists of unharmonized melodies structured with rhythmic cycles up to 48 beats.

The most celebrated literary figure in Lebanon is Khalil Gibran (1883–1931). He was a philosophical essayist, novelist, mystic poet, and painter. His most famous work was *The Prophet*.

The Lebanese place great importance on family life and are disarmingly open with strangers. Hospitality is inborn and generous. *"Ahlan Wa Sahlan"* is a welcome that embraces you as a friend and makes guests feel comfortable and relaxed. Coffee and appetizers (mezza) are generally offered with bread. Bread is considered the staff of life, and breaking bread together is an age-old tradition that signifies the sealing of friendships. To refuse to partake can be considered an insult.

Acknowledgments

There are many people I would like to thank for their help, encouragement, and inspiration. Creating a cookbook can be a humbling process, so I send my sincerest thanks and appreciation to all my family and friends for their patience and support.

I am grateful to my mother, Emma Kalush, for her patience and advice throughout this project. She has taught me most of what I know about Lebanese cooking and has contributed greatly with the history and old Lebanese traditions. Thank you, Mom, for the map, flags, village picture, other memorabilia, and artifacts incorporated into this book.

To Bobbie Johnson and Elaine Smith I extend appreciation for their editorial advice and helpful feedback.

I would also like to thank Kathy King, who guided me through the first steps of writing a book. She was instrumental in bringing me together with promoters, marketers, book designers, and graphic designers.

To all my many friends who were taste testers, my gratitude goes out to you for allowing me to share our foods and our culture. Also, a special thank-you goes to all those who convinced me that my concept of Lebanese cooking should become a cookbook.

I am grateful to several other family members. My sister Geri Sandborn-Conklin was a source for some recipes, a taste tester, and a constant support during the writing of this book. My sister Elaine Archer and my wonderful daughter Jamie Reavely provided help with the book title and encouragement. My Aunt Dorothy supplied a picture of my grandmother baking bread. My Aunt Jeannette gave me some of my grandmother's recipes. Special gratitude goes to my grandmother, who was with me throughout this endeavor in spirit.

Finally, my sincerest thanks goes to my husband, Blair Moore, without whose unflagging support, dedication, encouragement, and patience this book would not have come to be. Thank you for putting up with my crankiness during my kitchen fatigue spells. Thank you for your persistence in insisting that I get this book finished and your support throughout.

Introduction

In recent years, Lebanese cuisine has become extremely familiar in Western countries. The traditional dishes of the Middle East are internationally renowned. The most popular foods, such as yogurt (laban), kibbee balls, tabouleh, baklawa, grape leaf rolls, pita bread (kimaj), chick-pea dip (hummus), and many more, are available as take-outs from restaurants, deli counters in supermarkets, and Middle Eastern or Greek specialty food stores. Progress has allowed us to purchase ingredients prepared or partially prepared in jars, cans, or boxes for immediate use. This eliminates many of the tedious tasks of preparation our mothers and grandmothers had before us.

As the younger generation adapts to the American kitchen, much of the old tradition and history of the culture as well as cooking techniques are lost. With the cook of the future in mind, I wrote *Kibbee 'n Spice and Everything Nice*, with as many shortcuts as possible to make Lebanese cooking easy. Also included are nutritional values for recipes.

There are many more recipes than this book holds, and I have selected only those I feel will be used and carried forward by the generations. Unfortunately, many others will be forgotten in time as our culture becomes more sophisticated and incorporates Western ways.

Although I was not born in Lebanon, my grandparents on both sides of my family were. I have enjoyed Lebanese traditions all my life and have a great enthusiasm for Lebanese cooking. When I learned to cook, my mother and my grandmother used a "handful of this and a pinch of that." It took time for me to translate that into proper measurements for recipes. In doing so, I created, along with my good friend Dale Farhat, a spice mixture for kibbee, which is the national dish of Lebanon. This spice helps greatly to create the proper flavor and simplifies the making of this dish. I call it "kibbee spice," and it can be purchased from the address on page xvi.

The foods of the Middle East vary, as do their names, depending on the region or village from which one comes. Our family is from Deir Mimas, a small village in southern Lebanon, approximately 50 kilometers from the Mediterranean Sea.

My book will bring wonderfully healthy and tastily spiced recipes to your dining table with minimal effort for cooks with a busy lifestyle. To all of you who use and enjoy this book, *sallam di-yatik*, God bless your hands. With that, let's break bread together with the traditional toast: *Sahtayne*—to your good health!

Things You Should Know

Meat

Leg of lamb—boned and trimmed of all fat, ligaments, and gristle—is traditionally used for making kibbee and shish kabob (Laham Mishwee). Round steak, sirloin steak, or other lean cuts of beef are a good substitute.

Rendered Butter

Melt unsalted butter slowly and simmer for 15–20 minutes, evaporating most of the water. A golden liquid will rise to the surface, and the milk solids will sink to the bottom. Skim any foam from the top, pour the clear golden butter into a container, and discard the milky residue. When stored tightly sealed, rendered butter will keep for a year or more. It has a higher smoking point than regular butter because the milk solids have been removed. Therefore, it may be used to cook at higher temperatures. Rendered butter is sometimes called clarified butter or drawn butter.

Yogurt

Always save a small amount of yogurt as a starter for the next time. To avoid curdling or scorching yogurt during cooking, stir constantly in one direction. If you purchase plain commercial yogurt to use as a starter, make sure it contains live and active cultures, including acidophilus.

Syrup

Syrup should be cold when poured over hot pastries or hot if the pastry is cold. Hot syrup will make hot pastry soggy. If both are cold the pastry will not soak up the syrup properly. This applies to any desserts and cookies that call for dipping in syrup or other glazes. Syrup can be made ahead and stored in the refrigerator for several weeks. Bring to room temperature before using.

Lemon Juice

Always use fresh lemon if possible, although I keep lemon powder or granules on hand. These are wonderful for salads and make less work for the busy cook. They can be purchased from Rafal Spice Co., 2521 Russell St., Detroit, MI 48207, phone: 313-259-6373.

Walnuts

The best way to prepare walnuts is to grind them manually in a rotary grater. The oils in these nuts will quickly turn into nut butter if overprocessed in a food processor or blender. The rotary grater will yield a nice combination of pieces to use for cookies and pastries.

Mint

Many Lebanese homemakers grow and dry their own mint. The dried crushed mint in the spice section of your grocery store does not do the job. Because mint is an important part of Lebanese cooking, I recommend growing your own or purchasing fresh mint in the produce department. To dry fresh mint, cut the stalks and lay them out on newspaper for several days. Pull the leaves from the stalk, keeping them as whole as possible. Store in an air-tight container. When ready to use, crush the leaves in your hand and measure according to the recipe.

Pine Nuts

Toasting nuts enhances their flavor. Caution: if you spread them on a cookie sheet under the broiler, be very careful, as they will burn in seconds. You may sauté them in a skillet until golden brown, but they also will burn quickly when cooked this way.

Kibbee Spice

This spice includes all the spices you need to make kibbee, except the salt. It takes the guess work out of making this wonderful dish. It can be purchased from J. Lorraine Co., 6346 Lake Dr., Haslett, MI 48840, phone 517-339-1694.

Explanation of Values Used

The nutritional values are estimates only, and they should not be construed as anything else. They were derived by using Mastercook software, by Arion.

Calories are total calories per serving or in some cases per piece (unless otherwise noted).

Protein is measured in grams.

Carbohydrates are also measured in grams and should make up about 45–48 percent of your daily intake of calories.

Fat is listed as total fat and saturated fat. Total calories from fat should be limited to 30 percent of your daily intake of calories, and saturated fat calories should be limited to 10 percent.

Cholesterol is measured in milligrams and should be limited to 300 milligrams of total dietary intake per day.

Sodium is also measured in milligrams and should be treated with limitations if you are on a low-sodium diet.

Fiber content is measured in grams. The total dietary figure should include at least 25 grams of fiber per day.

Definition of Ingredients

Bulghur *(also called burghul)* Crushed wheat kernels, steamed, dried, and crushed, sometimes confused with cracked wheat, which is the whole wheat berry broken into fragments. Both come in a coarse, medium, or fine grade.

Hummus Chick-peas, garbanzo beans

Kishik Bulghur and laban mixture that is fermented, dried, and ground to a powder

Koosa Squash, small and light green in color. Zucchini is a good substitute.

Laban Yogurt

Mahleb Black cherry kernels, ground into powder

Malfoof Cabbage

Mazahar Orange blossom water, liquid extracted from orange blossoms

Na' na Spearmint leaves, fresh or dried

Roz Rice

Shiriah Vermicelli noodle or orzo pasta

Snoobar Pine nuts, found in the cones from some pine trees

Tahini Ground sesame seeds, made into a paste

Warek eneb Grape leaves

Zahtar Thyme and sumac, blended. A nonpoisonous variety of sumac is used, with berries that have a sour, astringent, not unpleasant taste. Their powder is brownish red.

Measurement Chart

3 teaspoons = 1 tablespoon

2 tablespoons = 1/8 cup

4 tablespoons = 1/4 cup

5 1/3 tablespoons = 1/3 cup

8 tablespoons = 1/2 cup

12 tablespoons = 3/4 cup

16 tablespoons = 1 cup

1/2 cup = 4 ounces

1 cup = 1/2 pint

1 cup = 8 fluid ounces

4 cups = 1 quart

1 cup uncooked rice = 3 cups cooked rice

Juice of 1 lemon = 3 to 4 tablespoons

1 medium onion, chopped = 1 cup

1 clove garlic = 1/2 teaspoon garlic powder

1 pound walnuts in shell = 2 cups, shelled

1/4 pound chopped walnuts = 1 cup

1 pound bulghur = 3 cups

6 oz. bulghur = 1 cup

1 envelope yeast = 2 1/4 teaspoons

4 oz. flour = 1 cup

1 pound flour = 4 cups

2 pounds flour = 6 cups

1 ounce butter = 2 tablespoons

1 pound butter = 2 cups

1 stick butter = 1/2 cup or 8 tablespoons

2 1/2 pounds rendered butter = 4 cups

1 1/4 pounds rendered butter = 2 cups

1 pound granulated sugar = 2 1/4 cups

1 pound pitted dates = 2 1/2 cups

1 pound apricots = 3 1/2 cups

1 pound cabbage = 4 cups, shredded

Appetizers

Avocado with Tahini

SERVINGS: 4

INGREDIENTS
1 large avocado
1 small clove garlic
2 tablespoons tahini
3 tablespoons lemon juice

Peel and mash avocado. Crush garlic and blend with tahini and lemon juice. Add to mashed avocado and blend until smooth. Salt to taste.

To serve
Use as filling for celery or hollowed out cherry tomatoes or as a dip for pita triangles, crackers, or pita chips.

DAILY VALUES

Total Fat	11.8g
Saturated Fat	1.8g
Cholesterol	0mg
Sodium	6mg
Carbohydrate	7g
Dietary Fiber	3.5g
Protein	2.5g

Percent of Daily Values
(2000 Calorie Diet)

Total Fat	18%
Saturated Fat	9%
Cholesterol	0%
Sodium	0%
Carbohydrate	2%
Dietary Fiber	14%
Protein	5%
Calories	132

Chick-Pea Dip

Hummus with Tahini

Cook chick-peas with liquid in saucepan for about 5 minutes to soften. Drain and reserve liquid. Put chick-peas in food processor or blender along with garlic, lemon juice, tahini, and salt. Add reserved liquid and blend until smooth. Thin with additional water to desired consistency if needed . Adjust seasonings to taste.

To serve

Place in shallow dish and drizzle with oil. This enhances the flavor and is a nice presentation. Garnish with lemon wedges and parsley.

Cut pita bread into triangles or use pita chips to dip into hummus. You can also use hummus as a dip for cut raw vegetables.

Shortcut

Hummus can be purchased in the can already mashed. All you have to do is add the lemon juice, garlic, and oil. It is available at Middle Eastern or Greek specialty stores.

SERVINGS: 6

INGREDIENTS
1 15 oz. can chick-peas
1 clove garlic
juice of 2 lemons
3 tablespoons tahini
1/2 teaspoon salt
1 tablespoon olive oil
lemon wedges
parsley sprigs

DAILY VALUES

Total Fat	6.8g
Saturated Fat	0.9g
Cholesterol	0mg
Sodium	298mg
Carbohydrate	11.3g
Dietary Fiber	2.3g
Protein	3.5g

Percent of Daily Values
(2000 Calorie Diet)

Total Fat	10%
Saturated Fat	5%
Cholesterol	0%
Sodium	12%
Carbohydrate	4%
Dietary Fiber	9%
Protein	7%
Calories	116

Eggplant with Tahini
Baba Ghanoug

SERVINGS: 6

INGREDIENTS
1 large eggplant
1 clove garlic
salt to taste
3 tablespoons tahini
2 tablespoons water
juice of 2 lemons
olive oil
pine nuts
parsley

DAILY VALUES

Total Fat	4.2g
Saturated Fat	0.6g
Cholesterol	0mg
Sodium	3mg
Carbohydrate	6.8g
Dietary Fiber	2.4g
Protein	2.3g

Percent of Daily Values
(2000 Calorie Diet)

Total Fat	6%
Saturated Fat	3%
Cholesterol	0%
Sodium	0%
Carbohydrate	2%
Dietary Fiber	9%
Protein	5%
Calories	68

Pierce the eggplant skin to let steam escape. Place the eggplant in a baking dish and bake for 45 minutes at 350 degrees until tender, or microwave for 5–6 minutes on high. The eggplant has a roasted flavor when cooked in the oven, so that is my preference.

When eggplant is cool enough to handle, peel and mash with a fork or in blender (but be careful not to liquidize). Crush garlic with salt; add tahini, water, and lemon juice gradually and blend until smooth. Combine this mixture with the eggplant, add additional salt to taste if necessary.

To Serve
Spread the eggplant on a platter or shallow dish. Drizzle with olive oil, garnish with pine nuts and parsley.

Cut pita bread into triangles or use pita chips to dip. This is also great with crackers or bread cubes.

Shortcut
Baba ghanoug can be purchased in a can already mashed. All you have to do is add the lemon juice, garlic, and oil. It is available at Middle Eastern or Greek specialty stores.

Yogurt Cheese

Gibnee

Crush and dissolve the junket tablet in 2 table-spoons cool milk or water. Heat 1 gallon of milk to lukewarm and add the dissolved junket tablet. Stir well and remove from heat. Cover and let set for 2 hours or more.

Break up the mixture with your hands and pour it into a strainer or colander lined with cheese-cloth; drain until all liquid is removed. With your hands, form flat rounds of cheese about 1 inch thick. Sprinkle with salt, cover with clear film wrap, and refrigerate. If cheese is to be used immediately, do not salt.

To Serve

This cheese is good for lunch or snacks with pita bread or crackers.

SERVINGS: 6

INGREDIENTS
1 gallon whole or 2% milk
1 junket tablet
salt

Fava Beans with Lemon

Fool m' Dammas

SERVINGS: 4

INGREDIENTS

2 cups fava or broadbeans,
  canned
2 cloves garlic
1/2 cup lemon juice
1 teaspoon salt
1/4 cup olive oil
2 green onions
1 lemon

Drain the beans and reserve liquid. Crush the garlic and combine with the lemon juice, salt, and oil in a small bowl. Mash beans with some of their liquid and add the garlic mixture.

To Serve

Transfer to a serving bowl and garnish with chopped green onions and lemon wedges.

Cut pita bread into triangles or use pita chips to dip into the beans.

DAILY VALUES

Total Fat	14.4g
Saturated Fat	1.9g
Cholesterol	0mg
Sodium	1166mg
Carbohydrate	34.1g
Dietary Fiber	3.9g
Protein	11.3g

Percent of Daily Values
(2000 Calorie Diet)

Total Fat	22%
Saturated Fat	10%
Cholesterol	0%
Sodium	49%
Carbohydrate	11%
Dietary Fiber	15%
Protein	23%
Calories	281

Pita Chips

Cut pita bread into strips about 1/4 to 1/2 inch wide. Heat vegetable oil in a skillet and fry the strips until golden brown and crisp. Fry in small batches so you can turn the strips for even browning as needed. Place the fried strips on paper towels to drain, and sprinkle with garlic salt while they are still hot.

Store in sealable plastic bags. When ready to use, put in a basket lined with a colorful napkin.

To Serve
Great by themselves, pita chips are even better when dipped in hummus or baba ghanoug. They are good with other commercial dips also.

SERVINGS: 6

INGREDIENTS
1 package pita bread
light vegetable oil
garlic salt

DAILY VALUES

Total Fat	0.1g
Saturated Fat	0.0g
Cholesterol	0.0mg
Sodium	53.6mg
Carbohydrate	5.6g
Dietary Fiber	0.2g
Protein	0.9g

Percent of Daily Values
(2000 Calorie Diet)

Total Fat	0%
Saturated Fat	0%
Cholesterol	0%
Sodium	2%
Carbohydrate	2%
Dietary Fiber	1%
Protein	2%
Calories	28

Toasted Pita Triangles

SERVINGS: 4

INGREDIENTS
1 package pita bread
1 teaspoon garlic powder
oregano
thyme
vegetable oil

Brush both sides of each pita bread with vegetable oil. Sprinkle with garlic powder, oregano, and thyme. Cut into wedges (6 or 8) and place on a baking sheet. Bake at 350 degrees for approximately 5–7 minutes or until crisp.

To Serve
Put in a basket lined with a colorful napkin. These are great with dips and spreads, such as hummus, baba ghanoug, yogurt, and commercial dips.

DAILY VALUES

Total Fat	0.7g
Saturated Fat	0.1g
Cholesterol	0mg
Sodium	322mg
Carbohydrate	35.5g
Dietary Fiber	1g
Protein	5.9g

*Percent of Daily Values
(2000 Calorie Diet)*

Total Fat	1%
Saturated Fat	1%
Cholesterol	0%
Sodium	13%
Carbohydrate	12%
Dietary Fiber	4%
Protein	12%
Calories	174

Pickled Turnips

Lift

Wash and cut the turnips in quarters. Pack turnips and beets in quart jars, using 2-3 beets per jar. Dissolve 2 tablespoons salt in 2 cups water. Add 1 cup vinegar and pour over the turnips to cover. Add 1 clove garlic to each jar; if you like them hot, add a teaspoon of hot sauce (optional).

Close the jars tightly and store in a cool, dark place. Turn jars upside down occasionally to blend flavors. Turnips will be ready in 2 weeks.

Option
Beets are used to give the turnips a pink color. Red food coloring can be substituted.

INGREDIENTS
10 whole small white turnips
1 15 oz. can whole beets
2 tablespoons salt
2 cups water
1 cup white vinegar
1 clove garlic per jar
Red hot sauce (optional)

Fried Cauliflower

SERVINGS: 4

INGREDIENTS
1 head cauliflower
salt
vegetable oil

Wash and trim cauliflower. Break or cut cauliflower into flowerets. Steam or parboil until partially cooked. Place on a clean paper towel to dry. Fry in hot oil until golden brown. Lightly salt and serve with yogurt or tahini sauce.

DAILY VALUES

Total Fat	6.9g
Saturated Fat	0.8g
Cholesterol	0mg
Sodium	7.5mg
Carbohydrate	1.3g
Dietary Fiber	0.6g
Protein	0.5g

Percent of Daily Values
(2000 Calorie Diet)

Total Fat	9%
Saturated Fat	3%
Cholesterol	0%
Sodium	0%
Carbohydrate	0%
Dietary Fiber	3%
Protein	1%
Calories	66

Soups & Stews

Chicken and Chick-Pea Soup

Shourabit Djaj il Hummus

SERVINGS: 6

INGREDIENTS

1 whole chicken—cut up
2 large onions
2 cups chick-peas, canned
1/2 teaspoon salt
1/2 teaspoon pepper
dash of cinnamon

Clean the chicken and put in a kettle with enough water to cover. Bring to a boil, cook for approximately 15 minutes, and skim the foam from the surface. Remove the chicken from the liquid and debone.

Cut the onions into wedges and add to the liquid along with the deboned chicken, chick-peas, salt, pepper, and cinnamon. Cook for an additional 25 minutes.

To serve
Sprinkle pita chips over the top or serve with fresh or toasted pita triangles.

DAILY VALUES

Total Fat	16.1g
Saturated Fat	3.7g
Cholesterol	123.4mg
Sodium	496.2mg
Carbohydrate	44.8g
Dietary Fiber	12.4g
Protein	53.4g

Percent of Daily Values
(2000 Calorie Diet)

Total Fat	25%
Saturated Fat	18%
Cholesterol	41%
Sodium	21%
Carbohydrate	15%
Dietary Fiber	50%
Protein	107%
Calories	585

Chicken and Rice Soup

Shourabit Djaj il Roz

Clean chicken pieces. Place in a kettle with water to cover, and simmer until tender, about 1 hour. Skim the foam from the surface, remove the chicken pieces from the liquid, and debone.

Chop the celery and add to the liquid along with the rice and seasonings. When the celery is almost tender, after about 15 minutes, add the chicken pieces and cook for an additional 25 minutes.

To Serve
Sprinkle pita chips over the top or serve with fresh or toasted pita triangles.

SERVINGS: 6

INGREDIENTS
1 whole chicken—cut up
10 cups water
1 cup celery
1 cup rice
1/2 teaspoon salt
1/2 teaspoon pepper
dash of cinnamon and allspice

DAILY VALUES

Total Fat	23.4g
Saturated Fat	6.7g
Cholesterol	140.6mg
Sodium	317.9mg
Carbohydrate	25.7g
Dietary Fiber	0.8g
Protein	31.0g

Percent of Daily Values
(2000 Calorie Diet)

Total Fat	36%
Saturated Fat	33%
Cholesterol	47%
Sodium	13%
Carbohydrate	9%
Dietary Fiber	3%
Protein	62%
Calories	449

Eggplant Stew

Batengen Yaghnee

SERVINGS: 6

INGREDIENTS

1 1/2 lbs. beef or lamb
2 large onions
2 tablespoons butter
1 large eggplant
1 cup water
1 28 oz. can diced tomatoes
salt and pepper
dash of cinnamon

Trim and cube the meat, and dice the onions. Stem, peel, and cube the eggplant. Sauté the meat and onions in butter until the onions are tender, add eggplant and 1 cup water. Cover and cook over medium heat for 15 minutes.

Add the tomatoes and cook uncovered for an additional 30 minutes, or until most of the liquid evaporates. Add salt and pepper to taste and a dash of cinnamon.

To Serve
Spoon the hot stew over cooked rice.

DAILY VALUES

Total Fat	34.2g
Saturated Fat	14.7g
Cholesterol	106.7mg
Sodium	366.3mg
Carbohydrate	8.3g
Dietary Fiber	3.0g
Protein	20.5g

*Percent of Daily Values
(2000 Calorie Diet)*

Total Fat	53%
Saturated Fat	73%
Cholesterol	36%
Sodium	15%
Carbohydrate	3%
Dietary Fiber	12%
Protein	41%
Calories	356

Lentil and Bean Soup

Shourabit Adas Mah Fasoolia

Rinse and sort the lentils. Put them in a large saucepan with about 2 cups of water and bring to a boil. Reduce heat and simmer for approximately 45 minutes. Coarsely chop the onions and sauté in the oil until golden brown.

Add the chick-peas, lima beans, kidney beans, onions, rice, salt, and pepper to the lentils; cook for an additional 30 minutes.

To Serve
Toasted or fresh pita triangles make good partners with this hearty soup.

SERVINGS: 6

INGREDIENTS
1/2 cup lentils
2 cups water
2 medium onions
1/4 cup vegetable oil
1/2 cup chick-peas, canned
1/2 cup lima beans
1/2 cup kidney beans, canned
1/2 cup rice
salt and pepper to taste

DAILY VALUES

Total Fat	9.8g
Saturated Fat	1.2g
Cholesterol	0mg
Sodium	321.9mg
Carbohydrate	40.5g
Dietary Fiber	9.4g
Protein	11.3g

Percent of Daily Values
(2000 Calorie Diet)

Total Fat	15%
Saturated Fat	6%
Cholesterol	0%
Sodium	13%
Carbohydrate	14%
Dietary Fiber	38%
Protein	23%
Calories	291

Lentil Soup

Shourabit Adas

SERVINGS: 6

INGREDIENTS
1 cup lentils
8 cups water
2 medium onions
1 cup celery
1 lb. ground beef
2 tablespoons butter
salt and pepper
1 lemon

Rinse and sort the lentils. Put them in water in a large saucepan. Bring to a boil, reduce heat, and simmer for 30 minutes. Chop the onions and celery. Sauté the meat, onions, and celery in butter. When the meat is browned, add the mixture to the lentils along with the salt and pepper. Cook until the lentils are tender.

To Serve
Squeeze fresh lemon over the top of each serving.

A basket of toasted or fresh pita triangles compliments this flavorful soup.

DAILY VALUES

Total Fat	24.3g
Saturated Fat	10.6g
Cholesterol	74.5mg
Sodium	303.mg
Carbohydrate	22.9g
Dietary Fiber	10.7g
Protein	22.4g

Percent of Daily Values
(2000 Calorie Diet)

Total Fat	37%
Saturated Fat	53%
Cholesterol	25%
Sodium	13%
Carbohydrate	8%
Dietary Fiber	43%
Protein	45%
Calories	156

Potato and Lentil Soup

Shourabit Batata Mah Adas

Rinse and sort the lentils. Put them and the water in a large saucepan; cook until tender, about 30 minutes. Dice the onion and potatoes. Sauté the onions in oil and add them to the lentils along with the diced potatoes, salt, and pepper. Cook until the potatoes are done and lentils are tender.

Variation

Sauté 1 pound of ground lamb or beef and add to the lentils when you add the potatoes.

To Serve

Serve with toasted or fresh pita triangles. Garnish with thin lemon slices.

SERVINGS: 6

INGREDIENTS

2 cups lentils
8 cups water
1 large onion
2 large potatoes
1 1/2 teaspoons salt
1/2 teaspoon pepper
vegetable oil

DAILY VALUES

Total Fat	0.7g
Saturated Fat	0.1g
Cholesterol	0mg
Sodium	642.6mg
Carbohydrate	44.4g
Dietary Fiber	20.5g
Protein	19.0g

Percent of Daily Values
(2000 Calorie Diet)

Total Fat	1%
Saturated Fat	1%
Cholesterol	0%
Sodium	27%
Carbohydrate	15%
Dietary Fiber	82%
Protein	38%
Calories	251

Stewed Eggplant

Imnazelee

SERVINGS: 4

INGREDIENTS

1 large eggplant
1 large onion
1 clove garlic
1/4 cup olive oil
1 28 oz. can tomatoes
1 1/2 cups water
salt and pepper
1 15 oz. can chick-peas

Peel and cut the eggplant into large cubes. Chop the onion and garlic and sauté in a pan with the oil. Place the eggplant, onions, and garlic in a large kettle. Add the tomatoes, water, salt, and pepper; bring to a boil and reduce heat to medium. Cover and cook for approximately 30 minutes. Add the chick-peas the last 5 minutes before serving.

Variation
Squash, potatoes, or both can be peeled, cubed, and added with the tomatoes.

DAILY VALUES

Total Fat	16.9g
Saturated Fat	2.2g
Cholesterol	0mg
Sodium	253mg
Carbohydrate	41.6g
Dietary Fiber	12.7g
Protein	11.8g

Percent of Daily Values
(2000 Calorie Diet)

Total Fat	26%
Saturated Fat	11%
Cholesterol	0%
Sodium	11%
Carbohydrate	14%
Dietary Fiber	51%
Protein	23%
Calories	351

Cold Yogurt and Cucumber Soup

Shourabit Khyar Ma' Laban

Chop the onion and garlic fine and sauté in the butter in a large skillet. Make 6-7 thin slices of cucumber before removing the skin and save them for garnish. Peel and slice thin the rest of the cucumbers and add them to the onion and garlic. Cook on low heat until soft, then remove from heat and stir in flour. Add chicken broth and stir well.

Transfer to a large saucepan and bring to a boil, reduce heat, and simmer for 5 minutes. Remove from heat and puree in a blender (small amount at a time). Cover and refrigerate.

To Serve
Stir in yogurt, salt, and pepper and garnish with reserved slices of cucumber.

Note: Other recipes for yogurt soup are given on pages 42–44.

SERVINGS: 4

INGREDIENTS
1 small onion
1 clove garlic
2 tablespoons butter
2 cucumbers
2 tablespoons flour
2 cups chicken broth
2 cups yogurt
1/2 teaspoon white pepper
1 teaspoon salt

DAILY VALUES

Total Fat	11.0g
Saturated Fat	6g
Cholesterol	31.0mg
Sodium	1566mg
Carbohydrate	15.3g
Dietary Fiber	1.7g
Protein	11.4g

Percent of Daily Values
(2000 Calorie Diet)

Total Fat	17%
Saturated Fat	32%
Cholesterol	10%
Sodium	65%
Carbohydrate	5%
Dietary Fiber	7%
Protein	23%
Calories	202

Yogurt Soup

Shourabit Laban

SERVINGS: 5

INGREDIENTS
3 cups yogurt
3 cups water
1/2 cup rice
1 egg
1 teaspoon salt
fresh or dried mint

Put yogurt and water in saucepan and stir to blend. Rinse the rice and add to the yogurt. Beat the egg, add salt and egg to yogurt, whisk to blend well. Cook over medium heat, stirring constantly until mixture comes to a full boil.

To Serve
Garnish with fresh or dried mint.

Note: Other recipes for yogurt soup are given on pages 42–44.

DAILY VALUES

Total Fat	115.6g
Saturated Fat	3.2g
Cholesterol	59.8mg
Sodium	507.3mg
Carbohydrate	21.3g
Dietary Fiber	0.2g
Protein	7.3g

Percent of Daily Values
(2000 Calorie Diet)

Total Fat	9%
Saturated Fat	16%
Cholesterol	20%
Sodium	21%
Carbohydrate	7%
Dietary Fiber	1%
Protein	5%
Calories	134

Salads & Dressings

Lebanese Combination Salad

Salata

SERVINGS: 6

INGREDIENTS

1 head lettuce

1 medium cucumber

2 tomatoes

2 green onions

1/2 cup parsley

1 green pepper

6 radishes

4 tablespoons salad oil

juice of 2 lemons

salt and pepper to taste

dash of garlic powder to taste

1 teaspoon mint leaves—dry or
   fresh

DAILY VALUES

Total Fat	10g
Saturated Fat	1.2g
Cholesterol	0mg
Sodium	56.5mg
Carbohydrate	14.2g
Dietary Fiber	4.9g
Protein	4.2g

Percent of Daily Values
(2000 Calorie Diet)

Total Fat	15%
Saturated Fat	6%
Cholesterol	0%
Sodium	2%
Carbohydrate	5%
Dietary Fiber	20%
Protein	8%
Calories	148

Clean and cut up vegetables as desired. Add oil, lemon juice, salt, pepper, garlic, and mint. Toss and taste, adjust seasonings as desired.

Sesame Seed Dressing

Tahini Dressing

Put the tahini into a bowl and add lemon juice, stir. Gradually add water until desired consistency is reached (about the same as bottled dressings). Add crushed garlic and salt. Taste and adjust for tartness and seasonings. Use this dressing for kibbee and falafel sandwiches.

Note: Nutritional values are for the entire recipe.

INGREDIENTS

1/2 cup tahini
juice of 2 lemons
2 cloves garlic
salt to taste
water

DAILY VALUES

Total Fat	16.3g
Saturated Fat	2.3g
Cholesterol	0mg
Sodium	271.2mg
Carbohydrate	8.6g
Dietary Fiber	1.8g
Protein	5.9g

Percent of Daily Values
(2000 Calorie Diet)

Total Fat	25%
Saturated Fat	11%
Cholesterol	0%
Sodium	11%
Carbohydrate	3%
Dietary Fiber	7%
Protein	12%
Calories	193

Tabouleh

Suff-Soof

SERVINGS: 6

INGREDIENTS

1 cup fine bulghur—#1 grade

2 bunches parsley

1 cup mint leaves—fresh

6 green onions

5 tomatoes

juice of 3 lemons

1/4 cup salad oil

salt and pepper to taste

Rinse bulghur and set aside. Wash parsley and mint, pull the leaves from the stems, and chop. Clean and wash vegetables and dice small. Add the parsley and vegetables to the wheat. Add lemon juice, oil, salt, and pepper and mix well.

To Serve

Use small tender grape leaves or lettuce leaves as scoops.

DAILY VALUES

Total Fat	11.4g
Saturated Fat	1.2g
Cholesterol	0mg
Sodium	110.2mg
Carbohydrate	40.7g
Dietary Fiber	7.9g
Protein	12.3g

Percent of Daily Values
(2000 Calorie Diet)

Total Fat	17%
Saturated Fat	6%
Cholesterol	0%
Sodium	5%
Carbohydrate	14%
Dietary Fiber	32%
Protein	25%
Calories	262

Lebanese Salad Dressing

Pour lemon juice and oil into a jar with a tight-fitting lid; add salt, pepper, garlic powder, and mint. Shake jar vigorously to blend. Taste and adjust according to tartness and seasonings. Refrigerate until ready to use.

Corn oil is a good substitute if a milder flavor is desired.

Note: Nutritional values are for the entire recipe.

SERVINGS: about 3/4 cup

INGREDIENTS
1/2 cup lemon juice
1/4 cup olive oil or vegetable oil
1 teaspoon salt
1/4 teaspoon pepper
1/4 teaspoon garlic powder
1 tablespoon crushed mint

DAILY VALUES

Total Fat	54.7g
Saturated Fat	6.3g
Cholesterol	0mg
Sodium	2135.5mg
Carbohydrate	11.9g
Dietary Fiber	0.6g
Protein	1.2g

Percent of Daily Values
(2000 Calorie Diet)

Total Fat	84%
Saturated Fat	32%
Cholesterol	0%
Sodium	89%
Carbohydrate	4%
Dietary Fiber	3%
Protein	2%
Calories	521

Lebanese Potato Salad

SERVINGS: 6

INGREDIENTS

6 medium potatoes

4 green onions

1/2 cup fresh parsley

1 tablespoon mint leaves—dried
    or fresh

juice of 2 lemons

1/4 cup oil

salt and pepper to taste

Boil, peel, and cube potatoes. Chop onions and parsley; add to potatoes. Crush mint leaves and mix with lemon juice, oil, salt, and pepper. Pour over cooled potato mixture and toss gently. Refrigerate until ready to serve.

DAILY VALUES

Total Fat	9.5g
Saturated Fat	1.1g
Cholesterol	0mg
Sodium	31.0mg
Carbohydrate	28.5g
Dietary Fiber	4.6g
Protein	4.7g

Percent of Daily Values
(2000 Calorie Diet)

Total Fat	15%
Saturated Fat	6%
Cholesterol	0%
Sodium	1%
Carbohydrate	10%
Dietary Fiber	18%
Protein	9%
Calories	207

Salad with Bread

Fettush

Toast pita bread until crisp. Break into bite-size pieces. Cut cucumber, onion, and tomatoes into bite-size pieces. Mix together with bread in a bowl. Add chopped parsley, garlic, salt, pepper, mint, lemon juice, and oil; toss well.

To Serve

Garnish with black olives. Serve immediately, or the bread will become soggy.

SERVINGS: 6

INGREDIENTS

2 pita breads
1 cucumber
4 green onions
3 medium tomatoes
1/2 bunch parsley
1/8 teaspoon garlic powder
salt and pepper to taste
2 tablespoons mint—dried
juice of 3 lemons
1/2 cup oil
black olives

DAILY VALUES

Total Fat	19.2g
Saturated Fat	2.2g
Cholesterol	0mg
Sodium	153.2mg
Carbohydrate	25.6g
Dietary Fiber	4.5g
Protein	5.9g

Percent of Daily Values
(2000 Calorie Diet)

Total Fat	29%
Saturated Fat	11%
Cholesterol	0%
Sodium	6%
Carbohydrate	9%
Dietary Fiber	18%
Protein	12%
Calories	283

Eggplant Salad

Batengen M'tabbal

SERVINGS: 4

INGREDIENTS

1 large eggplant
3 green onions
1 garlic clove
1 teaspoon salt
1/4 cup lemon juice
2 tablespoons olive oil
1/4 teaspoon pepper
1/2 teaspoon mint

Prick eggplant skin several times with a small knife. Place on a hot grill or in a 350 degree oven for approximately 30 minutes. (An open fire gives the eggplant a deep roasted flavor.) Eggplant should be soft to the touch but firm enough to cut into pieces.

Run the eggplant under cold water, peel, and cut into cubes. Place it in a salad bowl and add the thinly sliced onions.

Mash the garlic and salt together, and put the mixture in a jar with a tight-fitting lid. Add to it the lemon juice, olive oil, and pepper; shake vigorously to blend. Pour the dressing over the eggplant and toss. Allow to marinate for 1 hour before serving.

To Serve
Garnish with fresh sprigs of mint or parsley. Serve at room temperature.

DAILY VALUES

Total Fat	7.2g
Saturated Fat	1.0g
Cholesterol	0mg
Sodium	554.9mg
Carbohydrate	17.0g
Dietary Fiber	5.9g
Protein	3.4g

*Percent of Daily Values
(2000 Calorie Diet)*

Total Fat	11%
Saturated Fat	5%
Cholesterol	0%
Sodium	23%
Carbohydrate	6%
Dietary Fiber	24%
Protein	7%
Calories	131

Cucumber and Yogurt Salad

Laban Khyar

If using fresh garlic, mash with the salt and mix with yogurt. Peel and dice cucumbers. Add mint, salt, pepper, and cucumbers to the yogurt. Blend well, taste, and adjust seasoning as necessary.

To Serve

Serve in individual bowls or as part of mezza (appetizer). Garnish with fresh or dried mint.

SERVINGS: 4

INGREDIENTS

1/2 clove garlic (or 1/8 tsp.
   garlic powder)
2 cups yogurt
2 cucumbers
1 tablespoon dried, crushed mint
salt and pepper to taste

DAILY VALUES

Total Fat	3.9g
Saturated Fat	2.4g
Cholesterol	14.4mg
Sodium	56.3mg
Carbohydrate	9.8g
Dietary Fiber	1.2g
Protein	5.2g

*Percent of Daily Values
(2000 Calorie Diet)*

Total Fat	6%
Saturated Fat	12%
Cholesterol	5%
Sodium	2%
Carbohydrate	3%
Dietary Fiber	5%
Protein	10%
Calories	91

Cucumber and Tomato Salad

SERVINGS: 6

INGREDIENTS

4 tomatoes

2 cucumbers

2 green onions

1 tablespoon mint leaves—dried
    or fresh

juice of 1 lemon

4 tablespoons salad oil

salt and pepper to taste

dash of garlic powder

Cut tomatoes and cucumbers into pieces. Slice the green onions. Put vegetables into a large salad bowl and add mint, lemon juice, oil, salt, pepper, and garlic. Toss together, taste, and adjust seasonings. Chill.

DAILY VALUES

Total Fat	9.6g
Saturated Fat	1.1g
Cholesterol	0mg
Sodium	17.8mg
Carbohydrate	10.4g
Dietary Fiber	3.0g
Protein	2.4g

Percent of Daily Values
(2000 Calorie Diet)

Total Fat	15%
Saturated Fat	6%
Cholesterol	0%
Sodium	1%
Carbohydrate	3%
Dietary Fiber	12%
Protein	5%
Calories	128

Yogurt

The Story of Yogurt (Laban)

Laban has been called the "healthful and filling" food for centuries. It is considered a natural antibiotic and a dietetic for stomach ulcers. Known in the United States commercially as yogurt, laban is almost an essential in the daily diet of the people of the Middle East, who believe it keeps the digestive system healthy. Many Lebanese still make yogurt at home.

Laban is served as a side dish with meat pies (sfeeha), a lentil-wheat dish (imjaddara), kibbee, and grape leaf rolls (warek eenab). When it has the consistency of cream cheese, it is used as a spread on pita bread. Blended with green onion, garlic, or other spices of your choice, laban can be used to top baked potatoes or as a dip for veggies and chips.

Laban is the easiest food to make and only requires two ingredients, milk and culture (starter). Success in making perfect yogurt depends totally on having the milk at the right temperature. Always remove and save some laban for the next batch.

Homemade laban has a slightly sharper taste than commercial yogurt. To sweeten it, mix in a little honey and serve with fruit and granola.

Yogurt

Laban

Bring the milk to a boil over medium heat (until it poaches on top). When milk rises, remove it from the heat and pour into a glass bowl. Allow to cool until your little finger can be held in the milk to the count of 10. If you can keep it in longer, the milk is too cool and should be reheated.

Add a few spoonfuls of the milk to your starter to warm and thin it; stir until smooth. Pour this back into the bowl of warm milk and stir. Cover securely with plastic wrap or a lid that will seal tightly and set aside for at least 6–8 hours or overnight. When yogurt has set (consistency of pudding), refrigerate.

You can thicken the yogurt by removing the whey. To do this, after it is cold, fold a clean terry cloth towel and place it on the surface of the yogurt; cover the bowl securely and refrigerate. The towel will absorb the whey. Squeeze out the towel and replace it on the yogurt as many times as necessary to obtain the desired consistency, such as that of sour cream or spreadable cream cheese.

Homemade yogurt is great with kibbee and grape leaves. Add garlic or onion for a wonderful chip or veggie dip and topping for baked potatoes.

Shortcut
Put milk into a microwavable bowl and microwave for 30 minutes or until it poaches on top. Use a thermometer instead of your little finger to test the temperature (110 degrees). Continue with above directions.

* The starter (robi) can be saved from a previous batch, or purchase plain yogurt that contains acidophilus and yogurt cultures.

INGREDIENTS
1/2 gallon milk (2% lowfat or homogenized)
1/4 cup starter (robi)*

Yogurt Spread

Lebanee

INGREDIENTS

1 yogurt recipe
2 teaspoons salt

Pour yogurt into a cheesecloth bag. Suspend the bag from the faucet in the sink and let drain until yogurt has the consistency and texture of cream cheese. This will take approximately 8 hours or overnight. Remove yogurt from bag and place in a mixing bowl, add salt, and mix well. To prevent spoiling, cover with a little oil and re-frigerate in a covered container.

Serve as a spread with pita bread, meat or spinach pies, or herbed bread. Excellent as a side dish with many entrees.

Shortcut

Purchase commercially made plain yogurt and continue with the above directions.

Yogurt Balls

Labanee Makbouse

Allow yogurt to drain in the cheesecloth bag (see page 40) until it is firmer than cream cheese. Rub the palms of your hands with oil and make balls from the yogurt the size of walnuts. Place these on a clean cloth towel or paper towels for about 2 hours to remove more moisture, which will make them firmer. The firmer the better. Put balls in sterilized jars, cover with oil, and seal.

To Serve
Drain off oil, place on a dish, and sprinkle with mint for garnish.

INGREDIENTS
1 recipe Yogurt Spread (lebanee)
olive oil

Yogurt Soup

Shourabit Laban

SERVINGS: 6

INGREDIENTS

1 qt. yogurt (laban)
1 qt. water
1 egg
¼ cup rice
1 teaspoon salt

Put yogurt in a heavy saucepan along with water and blend until smooth. Beat egg. Rinse rice. Add egg, rice, and salt to yogurt. Stir. Place saucepan over medium heat, stirring constantly. Bring to a boil (be careful not to scorch). Reduce heat and simmer for approximately 20 minutes, stirring occasionally.

To Serve
Yogurt soup can be served hot or cold. Garnish with fresh or dried mint.

DAILY VALUES

Total Fat	3.8g
Saturated Fat	3.4g
Cholesterol	54.6mg
Sodium	441.1mg
Carbohydrate	13.3g
Dietary Fiber	0.1g
Protein	6.8g

Percent of Daily Values
(2000 Calorie Diet)

Total Fat	9%
Saturated Fat	17%
Cholesterol	18%
Sodium	18%
Carbohydrate	4%
Dietary Fiber	0%
Protein	14%
Calories	134

Yogurt Soup with Stuffed Dumplings

Sheesh Barrak

Filling

Brown pine nuts in a small amount of butter until golden brown. Chop onion fine and mix with ground beef, salt, pepper, allspice, and pine nuts.

Dough

Knead flour and baking soda with approximately 1/2 cup water and a pinch of salt. Roll out dough on floured board and cut into 2-inch rounds. Place approximately 1 teaspoon of meat mixture on a round; fold in half and seal edges. Wrap the dumpling around your little finger and pinch the pointed ends together, resembling a tortellini. Set aside until all are completed.

Yogurt Soup *(See recipe on previous page)*

Add stuffed dumplings at the same time you add the rice and cook for approximately 20 minutes, stirring occasionally. To serve, sprinkle with fresh or dried mint for garnish.

Note: The stuffed dumplings may be frozen for serving at a later time. Freeze them individually on a cookie sheet so they do not lose their shape. When they are completely hard, put them into a sack or container. To use, thaw the dumplings, or drop them frozen into simmering yogurt soup and continue heating for 10–15 minutes.

SERVINGS: 8

INGREDIENTS
Filling
2 tablespoons pine nuts
1 small onion
1 lb. coarsely ground beef (lean)
salt and pepper to taste
1/4 teaspoon allspice

Dough
2 cups flour
2 tablespoons baking soda
water
dash of salt

Yogurt Soup *(page 42)*

DAILY VALUES

Total Fat	16.8g
Saturated Fat	7g
Cholesterol	79.5mg
Sodium	1369.4mg
Carbohydrate	35g
Dietary Fiber	0.4g
Protein	19.2g

Percent of Daily Values
(2000 Calorie Diet)

Total Fat	26%
Saturated Fat	35%
Cholesterol	27%
Sodium	57%
Carbohydrate	12%
Dietary Fiber	2%
Protein	37%
Calories	380

Yogurt Soup with Kibbee Balls
Kibbee Labaneeyee

SERVINGS: 8

INGREDIENTS
Kibbee
1 cup fine bulghur (#1 grade)
1 medium onion
2 3/4 teaspoons salt
3/4 teaspoon kibbee spice*
1 lb. finely ground sirloin or
*   lamb*

Filling
2 tablespoons pine nuts
1 small onion
1/2 lb. coarsely ground sirloin
*   or lamb*
salt, pepper, cinnamon, allspice
*   to taste*

Yogurt Soup *(See page 42)*

DAILY VALUES

Total Fat	18.2g
Saturated Fat	7.6g
Cholesterol	83.5mg
Sodium	2185.3mg
Carbohydrate	56.7g
Dietary Fiber	3.8g
Protein	23.4g

Percent of Daily Values
(2000 Calorie Diet)

Total Fat	28%
Saturated Fat	38%
Cholesterol	28%
Sodium	91%
Carbohydrate	19%
Dietary Fiber	15%
Protein	47%
Calories	484

Kibbee
Rinse bulghur twice in cold water, drain, and cover
to 1/2 inch with fresh water to soak. Grind onion
(or mince in blender or food processor) very fine.
Add salt and spice to onion and mix. Add mixture
to ground meat and combine well with hands.
Squeeze any moisture from the bulghur and add to
the meat mixture. Knead together, adding cold
water as necessary for moisture. Make balls from
kibbee mixture the size of walnuts.

Filling
Sauté pine nuts and diced onion in small amount
of butter until onions are transparent. Add meat
and cook until no longer pink, stirring and
mashing to remove lumps. Add salt, pepper,
cinnamon, and allspice; taste and adjust seasonings.

Assembly
Poke a kibbee ball and press to hollow the center,
turning the ball in your hand. Keep hands
moistened with water while making the shell. Put
in 1 tablespoon of filling and close up the ball,
keeping it round. Set aside until all are completed.

Yogurt Soup
Start the yogurt soup. Add the kibbee balls at the
same time you add the rinsed rice. Cook for 15 to
20 minutes, stirring occasionally. Serve hot with
fresh or dried mint sprinkled on top for garnish.

* If you do not have kibbee spice, use the following: 1/4 tsp.
cinnamon, 1/4 tsp. allspice, 1/2 tsp. pepper. Kibbee spice may
be purchased from the address on page xvi.

Yogurt and Cucumber Salad
Laban Khyar

If using fresh garlic, mash with the salt and mix with yogurt. Peel and dice cucumbers. Add mint, salt, pepper, and cucumbers to the yogurt. Blend well, taste, and adjust seasoning as necessary.

To Serve
Serve in individual bowls or as part of mezza (appetizer). Garnish with fresh or dried mint.

SERVINGS: 4

INGREDIENTS
1/2 clove garlic (or 1/8 tsp. garlic powder)
2 cups yogurt
2 cucumbers
1 tablespoon mint leaves—chopped or crushed
salt and pepper to taste

DAILY VALUES

Total Fat	3.9g
Saturated Fat	2.4g
Cholesterol	14.4mg
Sodium	56.3mg
Carbohydrate	9.8g
Dietary Fiber	1.2g
Protein	5.2g

Percent of Daily Values (2000 Calorie Diet)

Total Fat	6%
Saturated Fat	12%
Cholesterol	5%
Sodium	2%
Carbohydrate	3%
Dietary Fiber	5%
Protein	10%
Calories	91

NOTES

A. Tabouleh Mix	D. Squash (Koosa)	H. Fava Beans	L. Tahini
B. Orange Flower Water (Mazahar)	E. Falafel Mix	I. Lentils	M. Halawa
C. Eggplant Dip (Baba Ghanoug)	F. Couscous	J. Broad Beans	N. Pickled Turnips (Lift)
	G. Grape Leaves	K. Chick Pea Dip (Hummus)	O. Yogurt (Laban)

These foods can be purchased from the following companies: Jerusalem Foods, 13080 Inkster Rd., Redford, MI. 48239, phone 313-538-1511 or Sahadi Importing Co., 187 Atlantic Ave., Brooklyn, N.Y. 11201, phone 718 642-4550.

Clockwise from top: Pita Chips, Eggplant Dip (Baba Ghanoug), Chick Pea Dip (Hummus), Yogurt Spread (Labanee), Plate with Sliced Tomatoes and Lettuce, *Center:* Pickled Turnips (Lift), Green and Black Olives (Zitoon).

Left: Lentil Soup (Shourabit Adas), *Right:* Chicken and Chick Pea Soup (Shourabit Djaj Il Hummus), *Top:* Lentil Beans

Clockwise from top: Cucumber and Tomato Salad, Tabouleh, Yogurt and Cucumber Salad (Laban Khyar).

Clockwise from top: **Pita Bread (Kimaj), Falafel Sandwiches and Lebanese Pizza, Open Faced Meat Pies (Sfeeha), Spinach Pie Triangles (Fatayer Sabanigh), Arabic Flat Bread (Khobaz).**

Clockwise from top: **Shish Kabob with Rice (Laham Mishwee Ma' Roz), Baked Kibbee (Kibbee Sineyee), Pine Nuts, Kibbee Footballs (Arras Mishwee), Kibbee Spice, Vegetable Patties (Falafel), Crushed Wheat (Bulghur).**

Top: Stuffed Squash (Koosa), *Bottom:* Grape Leaf Rolls (Warak Eenab),
Right: Baked Stuffed Eggplant (Sheigh Il Mihshee).

Counter clockwise from top: Lady Fingers (Baklawa Rolls), Jordon Almonds, Baklawa, Rice Pudding (Roz lb Haleeb), Plate of Butter Cookies (Ghrabee with almonds, cresent shaped and S shaped) Finger cookies (Makaroons) Nut-Filled Cookies with Powdered Sugar (Ma' Mool) Date-Filled Cookies (Ma' Mool bi Ajwi).

NOTES

Eggs

Egg Omelet

Ijee

SERVINGS: 4

INGREDIENTS

3 green onions

2 tablespoons vegetable oil or
   butter

6 large eggs

2 tablespoons fresh mint,
   chopped, or 1 tablespoon
   dried mint, crushed

salt and pepper to taste

Dice onions and sauté in oil or butter. Break eggs into a mixing bowl. Add mint, salt, and pepper; beat well. Pour eggs over onions and cook until golden brown on both sides. Also good scrambled.

To Serve

Good accompaniments are fresh sliced tomatoes, yogurt, and pita bread.

DAILY VALUES

Total Fat	12.4g
Saturated Fat	3.2g
Cholesterol	318.8mg
Sodium	646.7mg
Carbohydrate	9.8g
Dietary Fiber	3.0g
Protein	11.8g

Percent of Daily Values
(2000 Calorie Diet)

Total Fat	23%
Saturated Fat	16%
Cholesterol	106%
Sodium	27%
Carbohydrate	3%
Dietary Fiber	12%
Protein	24%
Calories	212

Scrambled Eggs with Squash

Ijet Koosa

Wash and dice squash. Sprinkle with salt and set aside. Dice onions and sauté in butter. Squeeze water from squash and add them to the onion; continue cooking until squash becomes transparent.

Break eggs in mixing bowl, add salt and pepper, and beat. Pour eggs over squash and onions; scramble to desired doneness. This also is very good as an omelet.

To Serve
Accompany with fresh sliced tomatoes and pita bread.

SERVINGS: 6

INGREDIENTS
2 medium squash
3 green onions
2 tablespoons vegetable oil or
   butter
4 large eggs
salt and pepper to taste

DAILY VALUES

Total Fat	8.0g
Saturated Fat	1.6g
Cholesterol	141.7mg
Sodium	45.3mg
Carbohydrate	2.6g
Dietary Fiber	0.9g
Protein	4.9g

Percent of Daily Values
(2000 Calorie Diet)

Total Fat	12%
Saturated Fat	8%
Cholesterol	47%
Sodium	2%
Carbohydrate	1%
Dietary Fiber	3%
Protein	10%
Calories	100

Scrambled Eggs with Tomatoes

Bayd bil Banadoora

SERVINGS: 4

INGREDIENTS

2 medium tomatoes
1 small onion
2 tablespoons vegetable oil or
    butter
4 large eggs
1 teaspoon salt
1/4 teaspoon pepper

Dice and seed tomatoes, set aside. Chop onion. Heat oil in skillet and sauté onion until transparent. Add tomatoes and sauté an additional 10 minutes to remove any moisture.

Break eggs in mixing bowl, add salt and pepper, and beat. Pour over onion and tomato mixture and scramble.

To Serve
Serve with fried cauliflower, yogurt, and pita bread.

DAILY VALUES

Total Fat	12.1g
Saturated Fat	2.4g
Cholesterol	212.5mg
Sodium	205.8mg
Carbohydrate	5.0g
Dietary Fiber	1.2g
Protein	7.1g

Percent of Daily Values
(2000 Calorie Diet)

Total Fat	19%
Saturated Fat	12%
Cholesterol	71%
Sodium	9%
Carbohydrate	2%
Dietary Fiber	5%
Protein	14%
Calories	155

Scrambled Eggs with Potatoes and Onions

M'farraket Batata Wa Bassal

Peel and dice potatoes. Heat oil in skillet, add potatoes, and sauté until tender. Add chopped onions and fry until potatoes are golden brown. Beat eggs, add salt and pepper. Pour over potatoes and onions, and scramble until eggs are cooked to your liking.

SERVINGS: 6

INGREDIENTS
4 medium potatoes
4 tablespoons vegetable oil or
   butter
6 green onions
6 eggs
salt and pepper to taste

DAILY VALUES

Total Fat	14.2g
Saturated Fat	2.6g
Cholesterol	212.5mg
Sodium	71.5mg
Carbohydrate	15.9g
Dietary Fiber	1.9g
Protein	8.3g

*Percent of Daily Values
(2000 Calorie Diet)*

Total Fat	22%
Saturated Fat	13%
Cholesterol	71%
Sodium	3%
Carbohydrate	5%
Dietary Fiber	7%
Protein	17%
Calories	222

Breads & Pies

The Art of Making Arabic Bread

The making of Arabic bread (*khobaz*) is indeed an art as well as a skill passed by mothers to daughters. As our mother began the task in the early hours of the morning, we would watch with wide eyes. After several minutes of kneading, she would divide the dough into several balls the size of grapefruit. She would let them rest for awhile, then pat and roll them out to the size of a dinner plate. She would then flip-flop the dough from hand to hand, a skill I have yet to master. The circle of dough grew larger and larger as it was thrown. It was so very amazing how she could catch it, toss it through the air with the greatest of ease, and catch it again, never missing a beat in this rhythmic motion.

Rose Abood (author's grandmother)

When the dough was larger than a pizza pan, almost two feet in diameter and paper thin, my mother would let it float gently down to a large wooden paddle dusted with flour. The bread was then placed in a hot oven on an iron sheet. It is so thin that it does not take long to become lightly browned and crisp. After taking the bread from the oven, Mom would stack one on top of the other until all were baked. She then sprinkled each with water and, when they were soft enough, folded them like a handkerchief. They were placed into plastic bags, six at a time, and refrigerated or frozen until needed. The bread is eaten by tearing off a small section and wrapping it around pieces of food, eliminating the need for a fork.

We called this Sito bread, the Arabic word for grandmother. Every time we visited our Sito, she baked bread, saving some dough to fry, which is a favorite of the family. As small children, we would ask Sito for some bread, which she would spread with butter or peanut butter and jelly and roll it up like a cigar. The name khobaz or Arabic bread were big words for us children, so Sito bread stuck.

The art of making this bread is becoming a thing of the past. My Aunt Dorothy has carried on the tradition and keeps the family supplied with the delicate bread. My younger sister, Geri, has been learning the skill of tossing the dough. Soon, she will be carrying on the tradition for the younger generation. This flat bread, as it is often called today, is produced commercially and can be purchased in some specialty food stores.

Basic Bread Dough

Fatayer & Talamee Dough

This basic dough can be used for meat, spinach, potato, and yogurt pies, herb and cheese bread, or talamee. Always add water a little at a time; the amount depends on the brand of flour you use. The key to tender bread is in the rising of the dough. It must at least double in size. The time this takes depends on the warmth of your kitchen.

Mix yeast with water and oil. Put flour in a large mixing bowl and add salt. Gradually add the liquid, mixing together to make a soft, *not stiff*, dough. It may be necessary to use a little more or a little less water, depending on the brand of flour.

Knead the dough until it becomes smooth and leaves the sides of the bowl. Form dough into a ball and cover with plastic wrap and a towel. Leave in a warm place to rise, about 2 to 2 1/2 hours.

YIELDS: 36

INGREDIENTS
1 package active dry yeast
1/2 cup vegetable oil
2 1/2 cups warm water
8 cups flour
1 teaspoon salt

DAILY VALUES

Total Fat	5.4g
Saturated Fat	0.7g
Cholesterol	0mg
Sodium	536.2mg
Carbohydrate	64g
Dietary Fiber	0.3g
Protein	9g

Percent of Daily Values
(2000 Calorie Diet)

Total Fat	8%
Saturated Fat	3%
Cholesterol	0%
Sodium	22%
Carbohydrate	21%
Dietary Fiber	1%
Protein	18%
Calories	346

Yogurt Cheese Pie Triangles

Fatayer Lebanee

YIELDS: 36

INGREDIENTS
Basic bread dough *(see recipe on page 55)*
1 medium onion
2 cups yogurt cheese (see recipe on page 5)
1 teaspoon vegetable oil
1/4 cup pine nuts
2 tablespoons butter

DAILY VALUES

Total Fat	5.5g
Saturated Fat	2.3g
Cholesterol	8.3mg
Sodium	222.2mg
Carbohydrate	21.7g
Dietary Fiber	0.2g
Protein	5.2g

*Percent of Daily Values
(2000 Calorie Diet)*

Total Fat	8%
Saturated Fat	11%
Cholesterol	0%
Sodium	8%
Carbohydrate	7%
Dietary Fiber	1%
Protein	10%
Calories	157

Roll dough to 1/8 inch thick. With a pastry cutter, make rounds of 3–4 inches and let rest. Chop the onion. Mix the yogurt cheese, oil, onions, and pine nuts. Preheat oven to 400 degrees.

Place 1 tablespoon of filling in the center of each round. Pull together two sides (one-third of the circle) and pinch up to the center, to make a raised seam. Do this two times more, leaving a raised Y on the top. Make sure to pinch dough tightly so it does not open during baking.

Place the triangles on a greased sheet and bake for 15–20 minutes, or until lightly browned on the bottom. Place them under the broiler to brown the tops if necessary. Remove from oven and brush with melted butter.

To Serve
These are delicious with salads or soups.

Shortcut
You can use cans of refrigerated biscuits. Flatten the biscuit with your hand and continue with the above directions. You can also use frozen white roll dough. Thaw and continue with the above directions.

Spinach Pie Triangles

Fatayer Sabanigh

Wash, stem, drain, and chop spinach. Place it in a large mixing bowl, sprinkle with salt, and let wilt. Squeeze the spinach until all the water is removed. Chop onions very fine. Add these to the spinach along with oil, lemon juice, and pepper. Mix well. Preheat oven to 400 degrees.

Roll dough 1/8 inch thick and cut into rounds of 3–4 inches. Put 1 tablespoon spinach filling in center. Pull two sides together (one-third of the circle) and pinch up to the center, making a raised seam. Do this two times more, leaving a raised Y on the top. Make sure to pinch the dough together tightly so it does not open during baking.

Place the filled triangles on a greased sheet and bake 15–20 minutes, or until bottoms are golden brown. Put triangles under the broiler to brown tops if necessary. Remove from oven and brush with melted butter.

Variation
Add 1 cup of crumbled feta cheese to the filling.

Shortcut
You can use cans of refrigerated biscuits. Flatten biscuits with your hand and continue with the above directions. You can also use frozen white roll dough. Thaw and continue with above directions. Canned or frozen spinach may be substituted for fresh, but make sure to squeeze out as much liquid as possible. These freeze very well.

YIELDS: 36

INGREDIENTS
Basic bread dough (*see recipe on page 55*)
2 lbs. spinach
1 1/2 teaspoons salt
2 medium onions
1/4 cup vegetable oil
1/2 cup lemon juice
1/2 teaspoon pepper
2 tablespoons butter

DAILY VALUES

Total Fat	3.4g
Saturated Fat	0.4g
Cholesterol	0mg
Sodium	318.2mg
Carbohydrate	22.9g
Dietary Fiber	0.9g
Protein	3.8g

Percent of Daily Values (2000 Calorie Diet)

Total Fat	5%
Saturated Fat	2%
Cholesterol	0%
Sodium	13%
Carbohydrate	8%
Dietary Fiber	4%
Protein	8%
Calories	137

Potato Pie Triangles

Fatayer Batata

YIELDS: 36

INGREDIENTS
Basic bread dough (*see recipe on page 55*)
2 lbs. potatoes
1 lb. beef or lamb
1 large onion
1/4 cup lemon juice
1 1/2 teaspoons salt
1/2 teaspoon pepper
2 tablespoons butter

DAILY VALUES

Total Fat	4.3g
Saturated Fat	1.2g
Cholesterol	8.5mg
Sodium	291.5mg
Carbohydrate	26.2g
Dietary Fiber	0.6g
Protein	5.9g

Percent of Daily Values
(2000 Calorie Diet)

Total Fat	7%
Saturated Fat	6%
Cholesterol	3%
Sodium	12%
Carbohydrate	9%
Dietary Fiber	2%
Protein	12%
Calories	172

Roll dough to 1/8 inch thick. Cut into rounds of 3–4 inches and let rest. Peel and shred potatoes and rinse in cold water. Squeeze out liquid thoroughly and place potatoes in a large bowl. Add coarsely ground meat, chopped onion, lemon juice, salt, and pepper. Mix well. Preheat oven to 400 degrees.

Place 1 tablespoon of the filling in the center of a round. Pull together two sides (one-third of the circle) and pinch up to the center, making a raised seam. Do this two times more, leaving a raised Y on the top. Make sure to pinch dough tightly so it does not open during baking.

Place the triangles on a greased sheet and bake 15–20 minutes, or until bottoms are lightly browned. Put triangles under the broiler to brown tops if necessary. Remove from oven and brush with melted butter.

Shortcut
You can use cans of refrigerated biscuits. Flatten the biscuit with your hand and continue with the above directions. You can also use frozen white roll dough. Thaw and continue with the above directions.

Note: You may place filling on one half of the round of dough. Pull the other portion over the filling to make a half circle. Pinch or flute edge and bake. These are easier and will look like a small version of a pasty or calzone.

Meat Pie Triangles

Fatayer Laham

Roll dough to 1/8 inch thick. Cut into rounds of
3–4 inches and let rest. Preheat oven to 400
degrees.

Lightly sauté pine nuts in butter until golden
brown. Mix together the coarsely ground meat
and browned pine nuts. Chop onions very fine.
Add onions, yogurt, lemon juice, salt, pepper,
cinnamon, and allspice to meat.

Place 1 tablespoon of the filling in the center of
each round. Pull two sides together (one-third of
the circle) and pinch up to the center, making a
raised seam. Do this two times more, leaving a
raised Y on the top. Make sure to pinch the
dough tightly so it does not open during baking.
Place the filled triangles on a greased sheet and
bake 15–20 minutes, or until bottoms are lightly
browned. Place under the broiler until tops are
golden brown if necessary. Remove from oven
and brush with melted butter.

Variation
Add a large tomato, seeded, peeled, and diced,
to the filling mixture.

To Serve
These are great with salads or cold yogurt and can
be served hot or cold.

Shortcut
You can use cans of refrigerated biscuits. Flatten
biscuits with your hand and continue with the above
directions. You can also use frozen white roll
dough. Thaw and continue with above directions.

YIELDS: 36

INGREDIENTS
Basic bread dough (see
  recipe on page 55)
1/4 cup pine nuts
2 tablespoons butter
1 lb. beef or lamb
2 medium onions
1/2 cup yogurt
juice of 1 lemon
2 teaspoons salt
1/2 teaspoon pepper
1/2 teaspoon cinnamon
1/2 teaspoon allspice

DAILY VALUES

Total Fat	7.9g
Saturated Fat	2.4g
Cholesterol	17.3mg
Sodium	343.5mg
Carbohydrate	22.2g
Dietary Fiber	0.3g
Protein	8.3g

Percent of Daily Values
(2000 Calorie Diet)

Total Fat	12%
Saturated Fat	12%
Cholesterol	6%
Sodium	14%
Carbohydrate	7%
Dietary Fiber	1%
Protein	17%
Calories	166

Open Faced Meat Pies

Sfeeha

YIELDS: 36

INGREDIENTS

Basic bread dough *(see recipe on page 55)*

Filling for Meat Pies *(see recipe on page 59)*

Roll dough to 1/8 inch thick. Cut into rounds of 3–4 inches.

Put 1 tablespoon of the filling into the center of each round. Flute edges and place on a greased sheet. Bake in preheated oven at 400 degrees for approximately 15–20 minutes, or until bottoms are golden brown. Place under broiler to brown tops, remove from oven, and brush with melted butter.

Shortcut

You can use cans of refrigerated biscuits. Flatten biscuits with your hand and continue with the above directions. You can also use frozen white roll dough. Thaw and continue with the above directions.

DAILY VALUES

Total Fat	7.9g
Saturated Fat	2.4g
Cholesterol	17.3mg
Sodium	343.5mg
Carbohydrate	22.2g
Dietary Fiber	0.3g
Protein	8.3g

Percent of Daily Values (2000 Calorie Diet)

Total Fat	12%
Saturated Fat	12%
Cholesterol	6%
Sodium	14%
Carbohydrate	7%
Dietary Fiber	1%
Protein	17%
Calories	166

Talamee

Cut and shape dough into 4-inch balls. Place the balls on a greased baking sheet about 2 inches apart, and flatten each to about I inch thick. Brush the tops with oil, cover with plastic wrap and towel, and let rise, about 1–2 hours.

Make a few dimples on the top of each round with your fingertips. Bake in a preheated oven at 400 degrees for 10–15 minutes, or until tops and bottoms become golden brown. Remove from the oven, cover with a towel, and allow to cool in their own steam.

To Serve
Tear this bread into pieces and eat with any meal. It is especially great with soups for dunking. For cheese bread, cut horizontally across the middle, brush cut surface with butter, and top with Swiss cheese. Put under the broiler until cheese melts. Cut into serving pieces.

YIELDS: 12

INGREDIENTS
Basic bread dough (see recipe on page 55)

DAILY VALUES

Total Fat	5.4g
Saturated Fat	0.7g
Cholesterol	0mg
Sodium	536.6mg
Carbohydrate	64g
Dietary Fiber	0.3g
Protein	9g

*Percent of Daily Values
(2000 Calorie Diet)*

Total Fat	8%
Saturated Fat	3%
Cholesterol	0%
Sodium	22%
Carbohydrate	21%
Dietary Fiber	1%
Protein	18%
Calories	346

Herb Bread

Zahtar Talamee

YIELDS: 12

INGREDIENTS
Basic bread dough *(see
    recipe on page 55)*
3/4 cup zahtar *(thyme and
    sumac blend)**
1/2 cup sesame seeds
1 1/4 cups vegetable oil

Divide talamee dough into 12 rounds (fewer or
more, depending on how large or small you want
the bread to be). On a floured board pat out
each round to 1/2 to 1/4 inch thick. Cover and
let rise for about 30 minutes.

Mix together the zahtar, sesame seeds, and oil to
make a paste. Spread the paste evenly on the top
of each round. Make 4–5 dimples with your
fingertips on top of each round.

Preheat oven to 450 degrees. Bake on a greased
sheet until bottoms are golden brown, approximately 10–15 minutes.

To Serve
Tear into chunks for dipping in hot soup or cut
as you would pizza and serve with lebanee
(spreadable yogurt). Cut into squares or triangles
and serve with any meal.

**Can be purchased at any Middle Eastern or Greek specialty
food store.*

*Note: If you want mostly talamee and only some zahtar, the
following is a per-bread recipe for zahtar: 1 tablespoon zahtar,
1 teaspoon sesame seeds, and enough oil to make a paste.*

DAILY VALUES

Total Fat	31.5g
Saturated Fat	3.8g
Cholesterol	0mg
Sodium	539.1mg
Carbohydrate	64.6g
Dietary Fiber	0.3g
Protein	10.6g

*Percent of Daily Values
(2000 Calorie Diet)*

Total Fat	49%
Saturated Fat	9%
Cholesterol	0%
Sodium	22%
Carbohydrate	22%
Dietary Fiber	1%
Protein	21%
Calories	584

Pita Bread

Kimaj

In a large mixing bowl dissolve yeast in water and add sugar. Let proof, then stir in salt and oil. Gradually add flour, mixing until dough becomes stiff. The amount of flour needed depends on the brand you use. Knead until dough is smooth and comes away from the sides of the bowl. Lightly oil the top, cover, and let rise until dough doubles in size, about 1 hour in a warm place.

On a floured surface, cut dough into 8 equal pieces. Roll each piece into a ball, then flatten with fingers to a round approximately 4 inches in diameter. Cover and let rest again for about 1 hour.

Roll each round to about 1/4 inch thick (roughly 6 inches in diameter). Cover and let rest for another hour.

Preheat oven to 500 degrees. Place each round on a heavy baking sheet or baking stone. Bake for approximately 5 minutes, until loaves balloon and become lightly browned on top. Remove from oven and cover with waxed paper and a towel, so breads will soften in their own steam as they cool. Press the tops down to flatten and store in plastic bags.

SERVINGS: 8

INGREDIENTS
1 package active dry yeast
1 cup water lukewarm
1 teaspoon sugar
1/2 teaspoon salt
2 tablespoons vegetable oil
2 3/4 cups flour

DAILY VALUES

Total Fat	3.9g
Saturated Fat	0.5g
Cholesterol	0mg
Sodium	135.7mg
Carbohydrate	33.9g
Dietary Fiber	0.4g
Protein	5g

Percent of Daily Values
(2000 Calorie Diet)

Total Fat	6%
Saturated Fat	2%
Cholesterol	0%
Sodium	6%
Carbohydrate	11%
Dietary Fiber	2%
Protein	10%
Calories	193

Lebanese Pizza

SERVINGS: 1

INGREDIENTS
pita bread
oil of choice
hummus* (pg. 3)

Lebanese pizza can be made from whatever you have on hand. Rub pita bread with garlic flavored, herb flavored, or extra virgin olive oil. Spread with hummus and sprinkle with basil or oregano. Add chopped, seeded tomatoes, chopped marinated artichoke hearts, and mushrooms. Top with crumbled cheese, feta or any other.

Bake at 350 degrees for 10 minutes, or until heated through. Cut in quarters and serve.

Use your imagination and create your own combinations. Thick pita bread is best for Lebanese pizza, which makes great appetizers and fun lunches.

* Can be purchased from your local grocer or at any Middle Eastern or Greek specialty food store.

Fried Bread

Thaw the frozen bread dough and place it in an oiled bowl. Rub the surface of the dough with a little oil, and cover with plastic wrap and a towel. Leave in a warm place to rise, approximately 45 minutes. Dough should double in size.

Pour oil, about 1 inch deep, in a skillet and heat to frying temperature. Pinch off a medium-size ball of dough (about 2 inches in diameter). Using oiled hands, flatten and stretch dough to resemble a long john (approximately 2 x 5 inches). Poke a hole through the middle to ensure even frying.

Drop the dough into the hot oil, fry until golden brown, turn, and fry the other side. The dough will puff up. Cook only enough at one time to fit comfortably in the pan. Remove from skillet and drain on paper towels.

To Serve
These may be sprinkled with granulated sugar, but the best way to eat them is to tear off a piece and dip it into jam, jelly, or maple syrup. This is usually a breakfast request from my children on weekends or holiday mornings.

Note: Fried bread is great by itself, but I sometimes serve with sausage links and juice. Yummy!

INGREDIENTS
1 package frozen bread dough
vegetable oil

Main Dishes

Kibbee

The national dish of Lebanon, kibbee is a highly seasoned mixture of finely ground meat, onion, and bulghur. It can be made in many forms, such as patties, ovals, appetizer-size balls, and loaves. It can be served hot or cold or raw, much like steak tartare. The meat may be lamb or beef. If you cannot find kibbee meat in a butcher shop or grocery store, purchase ground sirloin (97% lean, which is the leanest you can buy). This will work very well for all cooked kibbee recipes. Ask the butcher to regrind the meat to fine; it should be ground finer than hamburger. If you choose to prepare the meat yourself, it must be very fresh, lean, and trimmed of all fat, gristle, and ligaments. I recommend purchasing round steak rather than leg of lamb because it is much easier to trim. Once the meat is completely lean, cut it into chunks, and put through a meat grinder or food processor.

Crushed Wheat *(Bulghur)*

This staple ingredient in Lebanese cooking is an excellent source of protein and fiber. It can be purchased from stores that specialize in Middle Eastern foods or from health food stores. The Arabic name for crushed wheat is *bulghur*, sometimes referred to as burghul. Cracked wheat has a nutty flavor and comes in three grades: fine, medium, and coarse (sometimes called #1, #2, and #3). The fine or #1 grade is used in making kibbee. The #2 grade is used for making tabouleh, and the coarse grain is used for some boiled dishes.

Pine Nuts *(S'noobar)*

Pine nuts come from the cones of certain pine trees. The scales of the cone contain a hard kernel that houses the nut. The cone is dried to open the scales, and the kernel is taken out and cracked to harvest the nut. The Mediterranean pine nut is long, thin, and oval. It is considered to be the finest variety. North American pine trees produce a nut that is shorter and rounder; it is less expensive and less tasty. Pine nuts should always be roasted in the oven or sautéed to a golden brown to bring out the nutty flavor. You *must* remove pine nuts from the heat the instant they reach this color, as they will burn very quickly. Pine nuts are used primarily in kibbee filling (*housie*), meat pies, and some eggplant dishes.

Raw Kibbee "The National Dish of Lebanon"
Kibbee Nayee

Rinse the bulghur twice in cold water, drain, and cover to 1/2 inch with fresh water to soak. Grind the onion in a blender or food processor until fine, add kibbee spice and salt, stir to blend. Add the mixture to the ground meat and knead thoroughly by hand.

Squeeze any unabsorbed water from the bulghur and add the wheat to the meat. Knead until well blended, adding ice water as necessary to keep a very soft consistency.

To Serve
Place raw kibbee on a plate and shape into a round with a slightly flat top. Drizzle with butter or olive oil. Spread on yogurt (laban) or kibbee filling (housie) as a top dressing. This dish also can be served as an appetizer (mezza) with pita triangles or crackers, green onions, and olives.

* If you do not have kibbee spice, use the following: 1/2 tsp. cinnamon, 1 tsp. allspice, 1 tbls. dried mint (crushed), and 1 1/2 tsp. pepper. Kibbee spice may be purchased from the address on page xvi.

SERVINGS: 8

INGREDIENTS
2 cups fine bulghur (#1 grade)
1 medium onion
1 1/2 teaspoons kibbee spice*
5 teaspoons salt
2 lbs. finely ground beef or lamb

DAILY VALUES

Total Fat	20.3g
Saturated Fat	7.9g
Cholesterol	78.3mg
Sodium	1475.9mg
Carbohydrate	33.4g
Dietary Fiber	6.3g
Protein	28.8g

Percent of Daily Values
(2000 Calorie Diet)

Total Fat	31%
Saturated Fat	39%
Cholesterol	26%
Sodium	61%
Carbohydrate	11%
Dietary Fiber	25%
Protein	58%
Calories	427

Baked Kibbee

Kibbee Sineyee

SERVINGS: 24

INGREDIENTS
Kibbee Meat Filling
  (Housie)
1 large onion
1/4 cup pine nuts
*1 lb. lean beef or lamb (coarse
  grind)*
1/2 teaspoon pepper
*1/4 teaspoon each, allspice &
  cinnamon*
1 teaspoon salt

Raw Kibbee
(See recipe on page 69)

DAILY VALUES

Total Fat	14g
Saturated Fat	5.6g
Cholesterol	41.8mg
Sodium	523.5mg
Carbohydrate	11.7g
Dietary Fiber	2.3g
Protein	12.8g

Percent of Daily Values
(2000 Calorie Diet)

Total Fat	22%
Saturated Fat	30%
Cholesterol	14%
Sodium	22%
Carbohydrate	4%
Dietary Fiber	9%
Protein	25%
Calories	220

Dice the onion and sauté with the pine nuts in butter until onion is tender and nuts are golden brown. (Be careful not to burn the pine nuts.) Add ground meat and cook until no longer pink, stirring and mashing to remove lumps. Add pepper, allspice, cinnamon, and salt. Taste and adjust seasonings. Set aside to cool.

Divide raw kibbee in half. Pat one portion evenly in the bottom of a buttered 8 x 12 pan; layer the housie over it. Shape the remaining half of the raw kibbee into thin patties (hamburger style), and place these next to one another over the filling. Press their edges together, using a little water, to make a smooth top layer.

Cut into squares of two or three inches, and score the top of each with an X from corner to corner. Dot with butter and bake at 350 degrees for about 45 minutes or until bottom is done and top is browned.

To Serve
Serve with hot baked chicken and Lebanese salad.

Kibbee Footballs

Arras Mishwee

Make a ball of raw kibbee the size of a large egg. Holding it in the palm of your hand, use your index finger to burrow a hole in the ball. Press toward the sides to hollow the center and make a shell, turning the ball in your hand. If you should break the shell, patch it with a little kibbee mixture. Keep your hands moistened with water while molding the shell.

Fill the hollow center with some filling (approximately 2 teaspoons). Pinch the open end closed and gently shape into a football. Place the footballs on a buttered cookie sheet and brush with melted butter. Bake in a preheated oven at 350 degrees for 25–30 minutes, or until dark golden brown.

If you prefer, the footballs can be fried rather than baked. Heat enough vegetable oil to deep fry until dark golden brown. Drain on paper towels.

To Serve
Baked or fried footballs can be served hot or cold.

Shortcut
Make a thin flat patty from the raw kibbee (hamburger style) and place a heaping tablespoon of filling in the center. Bring up the sides and, with moistened hands, roll between your hands to shape into footballs. Deep fry or bake as directed.

SERVINGS: 12–15

INGREDIENTS
Raw Kibbee
(See recipe on page 69)

Kibbee Meat Filling
    (Housie)
(See recipe on page 70)

vegetable oil for frying

Burrowing a hole in the ball of a raw Kibbee.

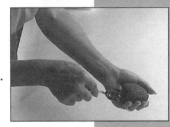

Filling the hollow center

Stuffed Kibbee Patties

Kibbee Arras

SERVINGS: 10–12

INGREDIENTS
Raw Kibbee
(See recipe on page 69)

Kibbee Meat Filling
  (Housie)
(See recipe on page 70)

Make thin patties from the raw kibbee. Put a heaping tablespoon of filling (housie) on one patty, add another patty to make a dome, and seal edges. Keep your hands moistened while working. The finished patties should be flat on the bottom and rounded on top.

Place the patties on a cookie sheet and brush with melted butter. Bake in preheated oven at 350 degrees for 30 minutes, or until brown on the bottom. Place under the broiler to brown tops if necessary, but watch carefully to prevent burning.

To Serve
Serve with salad or put inside pita pocket and top with salad for a tasty sandwich.

Unstuffed Fried Kibbee Patties

Prepare a half recipe of raw kibbee.

Make patties approximately 1/2 inch thick. Fry both sides slowly in vegetable oil until golden brown.

To Serve
Put each patty into a pita bread and top with salad and chick-pea dip (hummus).

SERVINGS: 6–8

INGREDIENTS
Raw Kibbee
(See recipe on page 69)

Unstuffed Fried Kibbee Balls

SERVINGS: yields 2 dozen

INGREDIENTS
Raw Kibbee
(See recipe on page 69)

Prepare a half recipe of raw kibbee.

Shape the raw kibbee into balls about the size of a walnut. Deep fry until golden brown.

To Serve
Put the kibbee balls on toothpicks and serve as an appetizer with hummus and yogurt for dipping.

The balls also may be cooked in yogurt soup, rather than fried.

Bulghur and Chicken

Imfalfalee

Debone cooked chicken and shred or cut into pieces. Rinse the bulghur and put it into a large saucepan with chicken broth. Add chicken, salt, and pepper. Cook over medium heat until bulghur is done, approximately 30 minutes.

To Serve

Spoon onto plates with a side dish of yogurt.

SERVINGS: 6

INGREDIENTS

1 cup cooked chicken
1 cup bulghur (#3 grade)
2 cups chicken broth
1 teaspoon salt
1/4 teaspoon pepper

DAILY VALUES

Total Fat	3.8g
Saturated Fat	1g
Cholesterol	31mg
Sodium	1480.7mg
Carbohydrate	35.2g
Dietary Fiber	6.6g
Protein	24.1g

Percent of Daily Values
(2000 Calorie Diet)

Total Fat	6%
Saturated Fat	5%
Cholesterol	10%
Sodium	62%
Carbohydrate	12%
Dietary Fiber	26%
Protein	48%
Calories	265

Stuffed Squash

Koosa

SERVINGS: 6

INGREDIENTS

6 small koosa — fresh or canned
1/2 cup rice
3/4 lbs. diced or coarsely
  ground beef or lamb
1 teaspoon salt
1/2 teaspoon pepper
1/4 teaspoon cinnamon
1/4 teaspoon allspice
2 tablespoons butter
1 28 oz. can stewed tomatoes
1 15 oz. can tomato sauce

Cut off the stem and hollow out the koosa (or zucchini) using a long corer available at specialty food stores. If you do not have one, you can use the pointed end of a vegetable parer or small spoon to scoop out seeds and flesh, leaving a shell with walls about 1/4 inch thick. Rinse the koosa with cold water and let drain.

Rinse rice and mix with the meat, salt, pepper, cinnamon, allspice, and butter. Stuff the koosa 3/4 full with the meat filling. Do not pack too tightly, so the rice has room to expand.

Place the stuffed squash in a saucepan and pour over it the tomatoes and tomato sauce. Add enough water to cover. Cover with a lid and bring to a boil over high heat. Reduce heat and cook for 45 minutes, or until rice is done.

To Serve
Place the cooked koosa in a serving bowl. Ladle the liquid into a sauce boat and serve on the side.

Shortcut
Koosa (unstuffed) can be purchased in a jar from Middle Eastern specialty food stores.

DAILY VALUES

Total Fat	17.5g
Saturated Fat	8.2g
Cholesterol	51.7mg
Sodium	681.7mg
Carbohydrate	20.2g
Dietary Fiber	2.7g
Protein	12.8g

Percent of Daily Values
(2000 Calorie Diet)

Total Fat	27%
Saturated Fat	41%
Cholesterol	17%
Sodium	28%
Carbohydrate	7%
Dietary Fiber	11%
Protein	26%
Calories	242

Hollowing out the seeds and flesh of the koosa.

Shish Kabob

Laham Mishwee

Trim and cut meat into cubes of 1 1/2 inches. Quarter onions and green peppers. Mix wine, lemon juice, oil, crushed mint leaves, and garlic for the marinade. Toss the meat, onions, and green peppers with the marinade. Cover and let stand for several hours (preferably overnight).

Prepare charcoal fire, gas grill, or broiler. Thread meat, onions, and green peppers alternately on metal or wooden skewers. (If using wooden skewers, first soak in water to prevent burning.) Season with salt and pepper just before cooking. Broil 10–15 minutes or grill over hot heat, turning once at the midpoint. Wrap pita bread around meat and pull out skewer, allowing bread to soak up the juices. Put into a covered dish until all meat is cooked.

To Serve
Serve with rice pilaf.

To make a sandwich, place cooked meat and vegetables in a pocket of pita bread and drizzle with tahini dressing or yogurt.

SERVINGS: 4

INGREDIENTS
2 lbs. beef or lamb
2 large onions
3 large green bell peppers
1/2 cup red wine
1/2 cup lemon juice
1/4 cup oil
1 tablespoon mint leaves
1/2 teaspoon garlic powder
salt and pepper to taste

DAILY VALUES

Total Fat	38.0g
Saturated Fat	16.6g
Cholesterol	125.9mg
Sodium	377.7mg
Carbohydrate	7.0g
Dietary Fiber	2.0g
Protein	30.8g

Percent of Daily Values
(2000 Calorie Diet)

Total Fat	58%
Saturated Fat	83%
Cholesterol	42%
Sodium	16%
Carbohydrate	2%
Dietary Fiber	8%
Protein	62%
Calories	648

Rice

Roz 'B Shiriah

SERVINGS: 4

INGREDIENTS

1 1/2 cups rice
1/2 cup vermicelli or orzo
1/4 cup butter
3 cups chicken broth
1 1/2 teaspoons salt
1/2 teaspoon cinnamon

Rinse rice and drain. Sauté vermicelli or orzo in butter until golden brown. Transfer to saucepan and add the rice. Add chicken broth, salt, and cinnamon; stir. Bring to a full boil, then reduce heat and simmer 15–20 minutes, or until rice is tender and water is absorbed.

To Serve
This is good with any chicken dish and a side of yogurt.

DAILY VALUES

Total Fat	13.8g
Saturated Fat	7.8g
Cholesterol	32.5mg
Sodium	2092.4mg
Carbohydrate	67.4g
Dietary Fiber	1.1g
Protein	14.5g

Percent of Daily Values
(2000 Calorie Diet)

Total Fat	21%
Saturated Fat	39%
Cholesterol	11%
Sodium	87%
Carbohydrate	22%
Dietary Fiber	4%
Protein	29%
Calories	459

Lentils and Rice

Imjaddrah ma' Roz

Rinse and sort lentils. Put them into a saucepan with the water; cook uncovered for 20 minutes. Sauté diced onions in the oil until dark golden brown. Remove from heat, add 3–4 tablespoons water, and mash with a fork. Pour onion mixture into lentils along with rinsed rice, salt, and pepper. Continue to cook over low heat until rice and lentils are done and water has evaporated, approximately 15 minutes longer.

To Serve
Good accompaniments are Lebanese salad and a side dish of yogurt.

SERVINGS: 6

INGREDIENTS
1 cup lentils
4 cups water
2 large onions
1/4 cup oil
1 cup rice
1 1/2 teaspoons salt
1/4 teaspoon pepper

DAILY VALUES

Total Fat	9.6g
Saturated Fat	102g
Cholesterol	0mg
Sodium	724mg
Carbohydrate	45g
Dietary Fiber	10.8g
Protein	11.6g

Percent of Daily Values
(2000 Calorie Diet)

Total Fat	15%
Saturated Fat	6%
Cholesterol	0%
Sodium	30%
Carbohydrate	15%
Dietary Fiber	43%
Protein	23%
Calories	230

Lentils and Bulghur

Imjaddrah

SERVINGS: 6

INGREDIENTS
1 cup lentils
4 cups water
1 cup bulghur (#3 grade)
1 1/2 teaspoons salt—level
1/4 teaspoon pepper
2 large onions
1/4 cup vegetable oil

Sort and rinse lentils. Put them into a saucepan with the water. Do not cover, bring to a boil, and boil about 10 minutes. Add bulghur, salt, and pepper. Cook diced onions in oil until dark golden brown. Remove from heat and drain any oil into the bulghur and lentils.

Add 3–4 tablespoons of water to browned onions and mash. Pour this into the bulghur and lentils. Stir and continue cooking until bulghur and lentils are done and water has evaporated, approximately 15 minutes longer.

To Serve
Serve with salad and side dish of yogurt.

DAILY VALUES

Total Fat	9.9g
Saturated Fat	1.2g
Cholesterol	0mg
Sodium	724mg
Carbohydrate	36g
Dietary Fiber	14.5g
Protein	14.3g

Percent of Daily Values
(2000 Calorie Diet)

Total Fat	15%
Saturated Fat	6%
Cholesterol	0%
Sodium	30%
Carbohydrate	12%
Dietary Fiber	54%
Protein	26%
Calories	223

Green Beans with Meat

Lubee Ah Laham

Wash beans, trim ends, and break in half. Cube meat and brown with chopped onions in butter; add salt, pepper, and cinnamon. Add the beans to the meat mixture, cover, and let steam for 10 minutes. Add tomatoes, tomato sauce, and water. Cook for approximately 1 hour over low heat, until the meat is tender and the sauce becomes thick.

To Serve
Serve over rice.

Note: I use round steak for this dish.

SERVINGS: 6

INGREDIENTS
2 lbs. green beans—fresh
1 lb. beef or lamb
1 medium onion
2 tablespoons butter
1 1/2 teaspoons salt
1/2 teaspoon pepper
1/4 teaspoon cinnamon
1 15 oz. can diced tomatoes
1 8 oz. can tomato sauce
1/2 cup water

DAILY VALUES

Total Fat	18.7g
Saturated Fat	8.3g
Cholesterol	60.9mg
Sodium	964.0mg
Carbohydrate	15.9g
Dietary Fiber	6.4g
Protein	17.5g

Percent of Daily Values
(2000 Calorie Diet)

Total Fat	29%
Saturated Fat	42%
Cholesterol	20%
Sodium	40%
Carbohydrate	5%
Dietary Fiber	25%
Protein	35%
Calories	292

Grape Leaf Rolls

Warek Eenab

SERVINGS: 10

INGREDIENTS

100 grape leaves—medium size
1 cup rice
1 1/2 lbs. beef or lamb (90%
*   lean)—coarsely ground*
1 tablespoon salt
1/2 teaspoon cinnamon
1 teaspoon pepper (scant)
1/4 teaspoon allspice
2–3 lamb or pork neck bones
6 extra-large grape leaves
1 cup lemon juice

DAILY VALUES

Total Fat	13.4g
Saturated Fat	5.8g
Cholesterol	41.4mg
Sodium	567.4mg
Carbohydrate	14.2g
Dietary Fiber	0.5g
Protein	10.3g

Percent of Daily Values
(2000 Calorie Diet)

Total Fat	21%
Saturated Fat	29%
Cholesterol	14%
Sodium	24%
Carbohydrate	5%
Dietary Fiber	1%
Protein	22%
Calories	222

If using fresh grape leaves, blanch in boiling water to soften and then run under cold water. Wash and drain rice. Mix the rice, meat, salt, cinnamon, pepper, and allspice. Place approximately 1 tablespoon of this stuffing across the wide end of the veined side of a grape leaf. Fold sides in and roll up. Do not roll too tightly, so the rice has room to expand.

Place the bones in the bottom of a large saucepan and spread 3 or 4 large grape leaves on top of them. Add rolled grape leaves in rows, crisscrossing each layer. Cover with the remaining large leaves. Place an inverted plate on the last layer to prevent rolls from floating.

Add the lemon juice and enough water to reach the plate. Cover pan and bring to a boil, reduce heat to low. Cook for 30–40 minutes, until rice is tender.

To Serve

Grape leaves can be served hot or cold with any dish and a side of yogurt.

Shortcut

Grape leaves are available in jars from Middle Eastern or Greek specialty stores.

Chicken and Rice Dressing

Hashwa

It is a Lebanese tradition to stuff a chicken or turkey with this dressing, but this method is not used much anymore. Today, hashwa is cooked on top of the stove and is served as a side dish with poultry. It is a must at all our holiday meals.

Melt the butter in a saucepan, add pine nuts, and stir until golden brown. Add meat and cook until no longer pink, mashing to remove lumps. Stir in salt, pepper, and cinnamon (adjust salt and pepper to taste).

Rinse and drain the rice, stir into meat mixture. Add the broth, stir once, cover, and reduce to low heat. Cook until all liquid is absorbed, approximately 20–25 minutes (or until rice is done.)

Note: Water instead of chicken broth or a combination of water and broth can be used to suit individual taste.

SERVINGS: 10

INGREDIENTS
1 1/2 sticks butter
2/3 cup pine nuts
2 lbs. ground beef or lamb, extra lean
1 tablespoon salt
1 teaspoon pepper
1 tablespoon cinnamon, plus 1 teaspoon
2 cups rice
4 cups chicken broth

DAILY VALUES

Total Fat	23.89
Saturated Fat	8.9g
Cholesterol	68.3mg
Sodium	1345.2mg
Carbohydrate	32.0g
Dietary Fiber	1.0g
Protein	26.6g

Percent of Daily Values
(2000 Calorie Diet)

Total Fat	37%
Saturated Fat	42%
Cholesterol	23%
Sodium	56%
Carbohydrate	11%
Dietary Fiber	4%
Protein	53%
Calories	449

Cabbage Rolls

Yabrak Malfoof

SERVINGS: 8

INGREDIENTS

1 head cabbage

1 cup rice

*1 1/2 lbs. ground beef or
    lamb—not too lean*

1 tablespoon salt

1/2 teaspoon pepper

1/2 teaspoon cinnamon

1/4 teaspoon allspice

2 tablespoons butter

3 tablespoons lemon juice

1 15 oz. can tomato sauce

1 28 oz. can diced tomatoes

DAILY VALUES

Total Fat	17.5g
Saturated Fat	8.1g
Cholesterol	54.9mg
Sodium	1122.3mg
Carbohydrate	28.8g
Dietary Fiber	1.2g
Protein	14.8g

*Percent of Daily Values
(2000 Calorie Diet)*

Total Fat	27%
Saturated Fat	40%
Cholesterol	18%
Sodium	47%
Carbohydrate	10%
Dietary Fiber	5%
Protein	30%
Calories	394

Core cabbage and parboil in salted boiling water until leaves become soft. Gently loosen leaves and remove them from the water with a fork or tongs. Put the leaves aside in a large bowl or strainer. When cool, cut the thick rib away from leaves and cut larger leaves in half.

Wash and drain the rice. Mix it with meat, salt, pepper, cinnamon, allspice, and butter.

Put a heaping tablespoon of the filling across a leaf lengthwise. Fold in the edges and roll up the leaf. Repeat until all are completed.

Place a rack in the bottom of a pan. Add the cabbage rolls in rows, crisscrossing each layer. Mix the tomatoes and tomato sauce; pour over the cabbage rolls, adding enough water to cover them. Add lemon juice and cover the pan.

Bring to a boil, reduce heat, and simmer for 30–45 minutes, or until rice is done.

Variation

Eliminate the tomatoes and tomato sauce. Instead, use I cup of lemon juice and enough water to cover the cabbage rolls.

Baked Stuffed Eggplant

Sheigh Il Mihshee

Cut off the stem and peel the eggplants. Cut in half lengthwise. Using a spoon or melon scoop, hollow out the center, leaving a wall about 1/4 inch thick. Chop the removed eggplant and reserve.

Sauté the pine nuts and chopped onion in butter. Add meat, salt, cinnamon, pepper, and the reserved eggplant. Cook until onions are tender and meat is no longer pink. Add about one-third of the stewed tomatoes to meat mixture and blend.

Place eggplant boats in a baking dish and heap in the meat mixture. Spoon over them the remaining stewed tomatoes and cook in a preheated oven at 350 degrees for approximately 30–45 minutes.

Variation
After removing the eggplant from the oven, top with grated cheese.

Note: If using a large eggplant, cut it into four pieces lengthwise, making wedges. Scoop out the top portion of each wedge to leave a canoe-shaped shell. Continue with above directions.

SERVINGS: 4

INGREDIENTS
2 small eggplants
1/4 cup pine nuts
1 medium onion
1 pound ground beef or lamb
1 teaspoon salt
1/4 teaspoon cinnamon
1/4 teaspoon pepper
1 28 oz. can stewed tomatoes

DAILY VALUES

Total Fat	32.2g
Saturated Fat	12.5g
Cholesterol	82.9mg
Sodium	906.5mg
Carbohydrate	21.1g
Dietary Fiber	6.8g
Protein	24.5g

Percent of Daily Values
(2000 Calorie Diet)

Total Fat	49%
Saturated Fat	62%
Cholesterol	28%
Sodium	38%
Carbohydrate	7%
Dietary Fiber	27%
Protein	49%
Calories	455

Fried Eggplant

Batengen Makli

SERVINGS: 6

INGREDIENTS
2 large eggplant
salt
vegetable oil

Cut off the stem and peel eggplant. Cut length-wise into slices 1/2 inch thick. Salt both sides of slices and layer them on paper towels, allowing them to sweat for about 30 minutes.

Heat oil in a skillet. Pat eggplant slices dry with paper towels and place them in the hot oil. Cook only enough at one time to fit comfortably in the pan. Fry eggplant on both sides until golden to dark brown. Drain on paper towels.

To Serve
Use as a side dish with any meal. This may be served at room temperature.

DAILY VALUES

Total Fat	0.3g
Saturated Fat	0.1g
Cholesterol	0mg
Sodium	4.6mg
Carbohydrate	9.3g
Dietary Fiber	3.8g
Protein	1.6g

Percent of Daily Values
(2000 Calorie Diet)

Total Fat	0%
Saturated Fat	0%
Cholesterol	0%
Sodium	0%
Carbohydrate	3%
Dietary Fiber	15%
Protein	3%
Calories	40

Baked Fish with Rice

Sayadiah

Rinse and dry fillets. Brown them lightly in butter and remove from skillet. Chop onions and cook with pine nuts in the remaining butter until golden brown. Transfer onions and nuts to a buttered 2 quart casserole dish. Top onions with the fish. Rinse rice and pour over fillets. Add salt, pepper, and lemon to the water and pour over all.

Cover and bake in preheated oven at 350 degrees for about 45 minutes, or until rice is cooked. Remove cover and bake an additional 15 minutes.

To Serve
Place fish and rice on a platter with lemon wedges for garnish. Serve with pita bread and Lebanese salad.

SERVINGS: 4

INGREDIENTS
2 lbs. cod fillet
1/2 cup butter
1 large onion
1/2 cup pine nuts
2 cups rice
1 teaspoon salt
1/2 teaspoon pepper
juice of one lemon
4 cups water

DAILY VALUES

Total Fat	34.9g
Saturated Fat	16.1g
Cholesterol	158.9mg
Sodium	1033.2mg
Carbohydrate	83.7g
Dietary Fiber	4.3g
Protein	52.3g

*Percent of Daily Values
(2000 Calorie Diet)*

Total Fat	54%
Saturated Fat	81%
Cholesterol	53%
Sodium	43%
Carbohydrate	28%
Dietary Fiber	17%
Protein	105%
Calories	406

Vegetable Patties
Falafel

INGREDIENTS
1 box falafel mix
vegetable oil for frying
water
Sesame Seed dressing
(See recipe on page 27)

These delicious vegetable patties have become so popular that they are readily found in restaurants and delicatessens. The falafel mix consists of chick-peas, potatoes, onions, garlic, salt, pepper, parsley, and sometimes fava beans. Because the powdered mix is available in Middle Eastern specialty stores, the chore of soaking the dry beans overnight and pressing the beans and potatoes through a food mill is no longer necessary. These make wonderful pita sandwiches.

Mix falafel according to package directions. Deep fry, making sure the patties are cooked completely through. When they are golden to dark brown, remove them with a slotted spoon and drain on a paper towel.

To Serve
Put 2 patties inside a pita pocket (either whole or broken in half), add diced tomatoes, diced pickled turnips (lift), and shredded lettuce. Drizzle with sesame seed dressing (tahini). This yummy sandwich is a meal itself.

Spinach-Filled Fillo

Sabanikh Bi Ajeen Baklawa

If fillo dough is frozen, thaw and carefully un-fold. Cover with a damp cloth or plastic to keep from drying out.

Wash and stem spinach. Chop the spinach and put in a large salad bowl. Clean and chop the green onions. Add these and crumbled feta cheese to the spinach. Pour over lemon juice and olive oil. Add salt and pepper, toss to blend. Taste and adjust seasonings if necessary. Beat the egg and pour over the spinach, toss again to blend.

Heat oven to 350 degrees. Grease a 9 x 13 glass baking dish.

Assembly
Melt the butter. Three sheets at a time, place 1/2 the fillo in the bottom of the baking dish, basting every third sheet with butter. Layer the spinach mixture over. Place the remaining 1/2 of fillo over the spinach, basting every third sheet with butter. Baste top sheet generously, making sure to reach the edges and corners to keep from drying out.

Bake at 350 degrees for 25–30 minutes or until golden brown. Remove from oven, allow to cool slightly, and cut into 3 x 3 inch squares.

To Serve
This is good with chicken dishes or shish kabob (laham mishwee) and tossed salad.

SERVINGS: 8

INGREDIENTS
1 package fillo dough
2 large bags spinach
4 green onions
1 cup feta cheese
1/2 cup lemon juice
2 tablespoons olive oil
salt and pepper to taste
1 egg
1/2 cup butter

DAILY VALUES

Total Fat	18.7g
Saturated Fat	9.9g
Cholesterol	69.8mg
Sodium	316.6mg
Carbohydrate	9.3g
Dietary Fiber	2.4g
Protein	4.9g

Percent of Daily Values
(2000 Calorie Diet)

Total Fat	29%
Saturated Fat	49%
Cholesterol	23%
Sodium	13%
Carbohydrate	3%
Dietary Fiber	10%
Protein	10%
Calories	215

Marinated Chicken

Djaj ma Limoon

SERVINGS: 4

INGREDIENTS

1 chicken—cut up
1 cup lemon juice
3 garlic cloves
1 teaspoon thyme
1 teaspoon basil
1/2 teaspoon cayenne pepper

Rinse and dry chicken pieces and place them in a bowl or resealable bag. Whisk together the lemon juice, crushed garlic, thyme, basil, and cayenne pepper. Pour the marinade over chicken and refrigerate for several hours or overnight, turning occasionally.

Place chicken pieces and marinade in a roasting pan, season with salt and pepper. Bake at 425 degrees for 50 minutes or until thoroughly cooked and golden brown. Baste occasionally.

To Serve
Garnish with sprigs of fresh mint or parsley and lemon wedges. Serve with rice (roz) and cauliflower or tabouleh salad.

DAILY VALUES

Total Fat	18.1g
Saturated Fat	4.9g
Cholesterol	185.1mg
Sodium	180.6mg
Carbohydrate	9.9g
Dietary Fiber	0.7g
Protein	60.7g

Percent of Daily Values
(2000 Calorie Diet)

Total Fat	28%
Saturated Fat	29%
Cholesterol	62%
Sodium	8%
Carbohydrate	3%
Dietary Fiber	3%
Protein	121%
Calories	452

Potato Kibbee

Kibbet Batata

Boil potatoes and set aside. Rinse bulghur and cover with water to soak.

Filling
Dice the onions, sauté with the ground meat and pine nuts; cook until the meat is no longer pink. Remove from heat and stir in kibbee spice and salt. Set aside.

Drain potatoes, peel, and cut into pieces. Place them in large bowl. Squeeze any liquid from the wheat. Add bulghur to the potatoes and mash together. Add salt, pepper, and egg, knead well; mixture should come together like soft pie dough. Add a small amount of water if necessary, for desired consistency. Butter 8 x 11 baking dish. Preheat oven to 350 degrees.

Assembly
Divide potato mixture and spread half on bottom of baking dish. Spread filling over. Top with other half of potato mixture. Dot with butter and bake for 30 minutes or until top begins to brown

To Serve
Cut into 3 x 3 inch squares and serve hot with a Lebanese combination salad (salata).

* If you do not have kibbee spice, use the following: 1/2 tsp. cinnamon, 1 tsp. allspice, 1 tbls. dried mint (crushed), and 1 1/2 tsp. pepper. Kibbee spice may be purchased from the address on page xvi.

SERVINGS: 6

INGREDIENTS
4 large potatoes
1 cup fine bulghur (#1 grade)
1/4 teaspoon pepper
1 teaspoon salt
1 egg

Filling:
1 lb. lean ground beef or lamb
1 medium onion
1/4 cup pine nuts
1/2 teaspoon kibbee spice*
1 teaspoon salt

DAILY VALUES

Total Fat	22.6g
Saturated Fat	8.6g
Cholesterol	90.7mg
Sodium	1040.3mg
Carbohydrate	37.3g
Dietary Fiber	5.9g
Protein	21.4g

Percent of Daily Values
(2000 Calorie Diet)

Total Fat	44%
Saturated Fat	52%
Cholesterol	40%
Sodium	30%
Carbohydrate	12%
Dietary Fiber	23%
Protein	44%
Calories	429

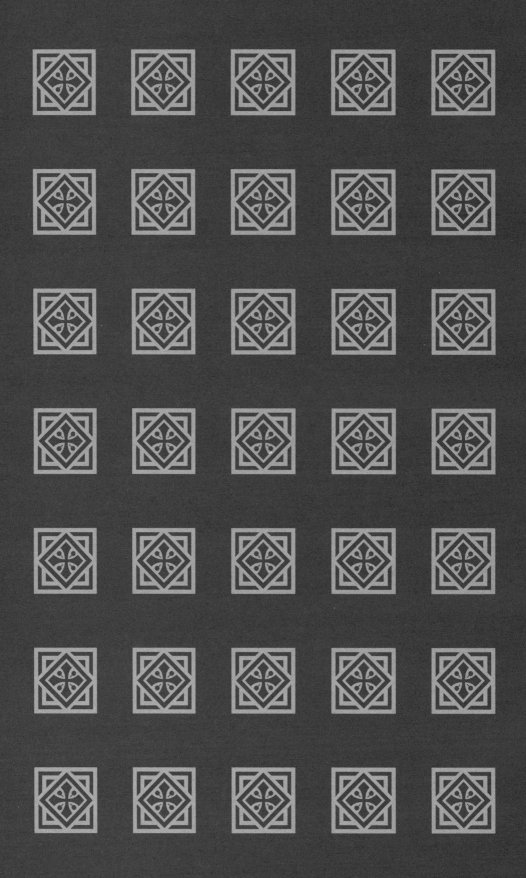

Beverages

[93]

Anise–Flavored Liquor
Araq

This clear alcoholic drink looks like gin. Araq is made from
sweet white grapes that have been crushed, then the juice is
distilled and flavored with anise oil. The liquor is poured
into small tumblers first, then ice cubes are added. If you
choose to add water to cut the strength, pour in the Araq
first and then add the water. It will immediately turn milky
or cloudy white. This drink tastes remarkably like Anisette.
Araq should be sipped.

Yogurt Drink

Pour yogurt into blender, add cleaned and rinsed fresh fruit. You can use any fruit, such as peaches, pineapple, pears, melons, strawberries, or other types of berries. Cut whole fruits into small pieces. Add the banana and crushed ice.

Blend until all fruit and ice have been incorporated. Pour into a tall glass and enjoy.

Variation
Add 2 tablespoons of protein powder for a wonderful healthy drink.

SERVINGS: 1

INGREDIENTS
1/2 cup plain yogurt
1 cup fresh fruit
1 banana
1 cup crushed ice

DAILY VALUES

Total Fat	4.8g
Saturated Fat	7.4g
Cholesterol	14.4mg
Sodium	62.1mg
Carbohydrate	42.5g
Dietary Fiber	6.2g
Protein	6g

Percent of Daily Values
(2000 Calorie Diet)

Total Fat	7%
Saturated Fat	13%
Cholesterol	5%
Sodium	3%
Carbohydrate	14%
Dietary Fiber	25%
Protein	12%
Calories	219

Turkish Coffee

Qahweh

SERVINGS: 1

INGREDIENTS

*1 teaspoon finely ground coffee
    per demitasse cup*

*1/2 teaspoon sugar per
    demitasse cup*

Cardamom

The offering of coffee is a part of the legendary hospitality of the Lebanese. Turkish coffee is purposely made strong and is meant to be sipped.

Put in a pan 1 demitasse cup of water for each serving desired and bring to a boil, add sugar. Add coffee, 1 teaspoon at a time, keeping water at a boil. Stir until it froths and add cardamom.

Remove from heat until froth recedes, then return to the fire. Repeat this procedure three times.

To Serve

Spoon a little froth into each cup. Let the grounds settle to the bottom of the pan and fill the cups with clear coffee. The froth will rise to the top.

DAILY VALUES

Total Fat	0g
Saturated Fat	0g
Cholesterol	0mg
Sodium	0.1mg
Carbohydrate	2.1g
Dietary Fiber	0g
Protein	0g

*Percent of Daily Values
(2000 Calorie Diet)*

Total Fat	0%
Saturated Fat	0%
Cholesterol	0%
Sodium	0%
Carbohydrate	1%
Dietary Fiber	0%
Protein	0%
Calories	8

Anise Tea

Shy ma' Yansoon

Bring water to a boil. Add tea bags and anise seed. Let steep for 10 minutes. Pour into cups and add a walnut to each.

SERVINGS: 4

INGREDIENTS
4 cups water
2 tea bags
1 teaspoon anise seed
walnuts—whole

DAILY VALUES

Total Fat	0.1g
Saturated Fat	0g
Cholesterol	0mg
Sodium	8.6mg
Carbohydrate	0.9g
Dietary Fiber	0.1g
Protein	0.2g

Percent of Daily Values
(2000 Calorie Diet)

Total Fat	0%
Saturated Fat	0%
Cholesterol	0%
Sodium	0%
Carbohydrate	0%
Dietary Fiber	0%
Protein	0%
Calories	5

Lebanese Tea

Miglee

SERVINGS: 4

INGREDIENTS

4 cups cold water

2 cinnamon sticks

2 cloves—whole

2 1-inch pieces ginger root

1 tablespoon anise seed

sugar to taste

walnuts

Put water, cinnamon, cloves, ginger, and anise in kettle. Bring to a boil and boil for 30 minutes. Add sugar and a walnut to each cup.

DAILY VALUES

Total Fat	1.5g
Saturated Fat	0.3g
Cholesterol	0mg
Sodium	23.4mg
Carbohydrate	15.5g
Dietary Fiber	6g
Protein	1.6g

*Percent of Daily Values
(2000 Calorie Diet)*

Total Fat	2%
Saturated Fat	2%
Cholesterol	0%
Sodium	1%
Carbohydrate	5%
Dietary Fiber	24%
Protein	3%
Calories	67

Desserts

Desserts

In the summer there is an abundance of fresh fruit in Lebanon, and it is served with coffee to finish a meal. Sweets are usually served late in the evening or between meals.

Most Lebanese pastries are associated with holiday seasons, religious ceremonies, and other special occasions. Many of the sweets from the Mediterranean region are very time consuming to prepare, and some are quite difficult to make. Fortunately, the most popular ones are available commercially.

Baklawa, the queen of desserts, is made of layers and layers of paper-thin pastry. It is filled with walnuts mixed with sugar or honey and orange blossom water and is prepared in a variety of shapes. The most recognizable are the diamond and lady fingers, or logs.

Epiphany is celebrated in the first week of the new year. Following evening services of the Orthodox Catholic Church, the parishioners honor this oldest of festivals by serving *zalabia,* which are similar to doughnuts.

Ma'mool and *kiak* are cookies that are Easter specialties, along with the traditional hard-boiled egg. Kaik and Easter eggs are symbolic of breaking fast.

Baklawa

Unwrap and carefully unfold thawed fillo dough; cover with plastic wrap or wax paper and a damp cloth to keep the dough from drying out.

Filling
Grind the walnuts coarsely, mix with sugar and orange blossom water until well blended. Butter a 12 x 16 inch baking pan. Render the butter.

Assembly
Layer one package of the fillo sheets in the pan, buttering generously between each sheet with a pastry brush or cloth dipped in butter. Mix 2–3 tablespoons of water with the walnut mixture and put over the top of the last sheet, making sure to keep the layer of walnuts level.

Repeat the same procedure with the second package of dough, buttering generously between each sheet, and butter the top. Cut into diamonds, dipping the knife into hot water as you go for easier cutting. Pour over any remaining butter.

Bake at 350 degrees for 45 minutes to 1 hour (depending on your oven) or until bottom is done and top is golden brown. If top does not brown nicely, put the baklawa under the broiler for a few seconds, watching constantly, as it will burn very quickly.

(continued on next page)

SERVINGS: 60

INGREDIENTS
2 packages fillo dough

Filling
2 lbs. walnuts
3/4 cup sugar
*2 tablespoons orange blossom
    water (Mazahar)**
2 1/2 lbs. butter

Syrup
3 cups sugar
2 cups water
*2 tablespoons orange blossom
    water*
2 tablespoons lemon juice

DAILY VALUES

Total Fat	24.0g
Saturated Fat	10.1g
Cholesterol	44.4mg
Sodium	159.9mg
Carbohydrate	14.7g
Dietary Fiber	0.8g
Protein	3.9g

*Percent of Daily Values
(2000 Calorie Diet)*

Total Fat	37%
Saturated Fat	51%
Cholesterol	14%
Sodium	7%
Carbohydrate	5%
Dietary Fiber	3%
Protein	8%
Calories	278

Baklawa *(continued)*

Syrup
Mix sugar and water together and bring to a boil. Boil about 15-20 minutes. Remove syrup from heat, add lemon juice and orange blossom water. Stir and let cool.

Tip
Syrup must either be cool and poured over hot baklawa or hot and poured over cooled baklawa. Never pour hot syrup over hot baklawa; it will make it soggy.

Shortcut
Butter pan and place one whole package of fillo dough in pan, butter top, and add nut filling. Place second package of fillo dough over nuts and butter the top. Cut into diamonds and pour all the rendered butter into the pan, making sure it settles into all the cuts and around edges. Bake as directed above.

* Can be purchased at any Middle Eastern or Greek specialty store.

Lady Fingers
Baklawa Rolls

Filling
Grind the nuts, mix with the sugar and orange blossom water. Render the butter.

Syrup
Bring the water and sugar to a boil, reduce heat, and simmer for 15 minutes. Set aside and let cool.

Assembly
Thaw and carefully unwrap fillo dough. Place plastic wrap and damp cloth over fillo to keep it from drying out. Lay 5 sheets on a clean surface, brush with melted butter. Place approximately 1 cup of walnut filling along the long side of the fillo pastry. Fold the sides toward the center and roll fillo, jelly roll fashion. Lay seam side down on a buttered baking tray. Repeat this process until all the dough and filling are used. Cut the pastry across, making pieces approximately 2 inches long. Pour any remaining butter over the cut lady fingers.

Bake in a preheated oven at 350 degrees for 30–45 minutes, until bottoms are golden brown. Place lady fingers under the broiler, watching constantly, until tops are golden brown. Do not leave unattended, as they will burn very quickly. Pour cooled syrup over hot lady fingers. Let set for several hours or overnight (unrefrigerated) to absorb syrup.

* Can be purchased at Middle Eastern and Greek specialty stores.

SERVINGS: 60

INGREDIENTS
Filling
1 lb. walnuts
1/2 cup sugar
1 tablespoon orange blossom water (Mazahar)*

Syrup
1 cup water
2 cups sugar
1 teaspoon orange blossom water

1 package fillo dough
1 1/4 pounds butter

DAILY VALUES

Total Fat	12g
Saturated Fat	5.1g
Cholesterol	20.7mg
Sodium	78.5mg
Carbohydrate	9.3g
Dietary Fiber	0.4g
Protein	1.9g

Percent of Daily Values
(2000 Calorie Diet)

Total Fat	18%
Saturated Fat	25%
Cholesterol	7%
Sodium	3%
Carbohydrate	3%
Dietary Fiber	2%
Protein	4%
Calories	147

Nut-Filled Cookies

Ma'mool

SERVINGS: 25

INGREDIENTS
Dough
*2 sticks butter (reserve 1
    tablespoon for filling)*
1 egg
1 tablespoon whiskey—optional
2 tablespoons milk
1/2 cup sugar
3 cups flour

Filling
1/2 pound walnuts
1/4 cup sugar
1 teaspoon butter
*1 teaspoon orange blossom
    water (Mazahar)**

DAILY VALUES

Total Fat	6.4g
Saturated Fat	1.0g
Cholesterol	11.0mg
Sodium	12.2mg
Carbohydrate	18.6g
Dietary Fiber	0.5g
Protein	4.0g

*Percent of Daily Values
(2000 Calorie Diet)*

Total Fat	10%
Saturated Fat	5%
Cholesterol	4%
Sodium	1%
Carbohydrate	6%
Dietary Fiber	2%
Protein	8%
Calories	200

Dough
Render butter and set aside to cool (reserve 1
tablespoon for filling). Beat egg, add to cooled
butter, and stir to blend. Add whiskey and milk.
Mix sugar with flour. Work flour and liquids
together into a dough. Cover and let rest while
making the filling.

Filling
Grind walnuts coarsely and place in a bowl with
sugar, butter, and orange blossom water. Blend
well and set aside.

Assembly
Form dough into small balls approximately 2
inches in diameter. Make a well in the center of
each with your finger, pressing against the sides
as you turn the ball to make a shell. Fill the
hollow with 1 teaspoon of the walnut mixture.
Pinch the opening closed.

If using a ma'mool mold, dust it with flour and
place the filled ball in the mold, unpinched side
down. Press dough gently into the grooves to
transfer the design onto the cookie. Do not press
too hard or it will be difficult to release the
dough. Tap mold to remove the cookie and place
it on an ungreased baking sheet. Clean the mold
occasionally, as the flour and dough may build
up in the grooves.

If you do not have a mold, shape cookies into a dome with a flat bottom and rounded top. Place the cookies pinched side down onto a cookie sheet and bake as directed.

Place baking sheet on the middle rack of a pre-heated oven. Bake at 350 degrees for approximately 12–15 minutes or until bottoms are golden brown. Sprinkle with powdered sugar when cookies have cooled.

Note: Ma'mool molds are available at any Middle Eastern specialty store.

* Can be purchased at Middle Eastern and Greek specialty stores.

Date-Filled Cookies

Ma'mool bi Ajwi

SERVINGS: 25

INGREDIENTS
2 tablespoons butter
1/2 pound dates
1/4 cup walnuts

Nut-Filled Cookies *(see recipe on page 106)*

Render butter in a saucepan. Chop the dates. Finely chop the walnuts. Over low heat, add the dates to the butter. Stir, breaking up date pieces and cooking them until soft. Add nuts and remove from heat.

Make dough balls, approximately 2 inches in diameter, and follow directions for Nut-Filled Cookies (page 106) to form a shell. Place 1 teaspoon of the date filling in each shell. Pinch the opening closed.

Place baking sheet on the middle rack of a pre-heated oven. Bake at 350 degrees for approximately 12–15 minutes or until bottoms are golden brown.

DAILY VALUES

Total Fat	2.9g
Saturated Fat	1.3g
Cholesterol	13.4mg
Sodium	21.7mg
Carbohydrate	22.3g
Dietary Fiber	0.7g
Protein	2.3g

Percent of Daily Values
(2000 Calorie Diet)

Total Fat	4%
Saturated Fat	6%
Cholesterol	4%
Sodium	1%
Carbohydrate	7%
Dietary Fiber	3%
Protein	5%
Calories	123

Butter Cookie

Ghrabee

Render the butter and chill it until it begins to set. Beat butter on high speed of electric mixer until it becomes fluffy. Mix the sugar and flour, gradually add this to the butter, and beat until the mixture is too heavy for the machine. Incorporate by hand the remaining flour and sugar.

Chill the dough for approximately 10 minutes. Take a small amount and shape into a ball the size of a walnut. Flatten slightly and press an almond into the center. Repeat until all dough is used.

Place cookies on an ungreased sheet and bake in a preheated oven at 300 degrees for 20–25 minutes. DO NOT OVERBAKE. Cookies should remain white, and the bottoms should be very lightly brown. Do not remove cookies from the sheet until they are completely cooled.

Variation
These cookies can be shaped into a crescent or S. Ground almonds can be added to the dough.

SERVINGS: 30

INGREDIENTS
1 cup butter
1 cup powdered sugar
2 cups flour
blanched almonds—halved

DAILY VALUES

Total Fat	6.1g
Saturated Fat	3.8g
Cholesterol	16.4mg
Sodium	61.9mg
Carbohydrate	10.4g
Dietary Fiber	0g
Protein	0.9g

Percent of Daily Values
(2000 Calorie Diet)

Total Fat	9%
Saturated Fat	19%
Cholesterol	5%
Sodium	3%
Carbohydrate	3%
Dietary Fiber	0%
Protein	2%
Calories	99

Date Roll

SERVINGS: 60

INGREDIENTS
Dough
2 cups butter
3/4 cup sugar
2 eggs
1 ounce whiskey—optional
1 teaspoon mahleb*
1 teaspoon orange blossom
   water (Mazahar)*
5 cups flour
water

Filling
1/4 cup butter
2 lbs. dates
3/4 cup walnuts

DAILY VALUES

Total Fat	8.0g
Saturated Fat	4.4g
Cholesterol	25.5mg
Sodium	72.2mg
Carbohydrate	21.8g
Dietary Fiber	1.2g
Protein	2.0g

Percent of Daily Values
(2000 Calorie Diet)

Total Fat	10%
Saturated Fat	17%
Cholesterol	8%
Sodium	3%
Carbohydrate	6%
Dietary Fiber	4%
Protein	3%
Calories	163

Dough

Render the butter and let cool. Cream it with the sugar. Add eggs, whiskey, mahleb, and orange blossom water. Stir to blend. Add flour gradually, kneading thoroughly. Add just enough water to make a dough of smooth consistency that does not stick to your hands. Cover and set aside for about 2 hours.

Filling

Render the butter and let cool. Finely grind the dates and walnuts together. Add butter and mix.

Assembly

Divide dough into four equal parts. Roll out one part at a time, on floured surface, to 1/4 inch thick. Spread with one-quarter of the date filling and roll up like a jelly roll. Place each log on an ungreased baking sheet. Make diagonal cuts across the logs approximately 1/2 to 1 inch apart, being careful not to cut all the way through.

Bake in a preheated oven at 400 degrees for 35–40 minutes. Place rolls under the broiler for a few seconds to brown top, if necessary. When cool, slice through and sprinkle with powdered sugar.

* Can be purchased at Middle Eastern and Greek specialty stores.

Finger Cookies

Makaroons

Dough

Grind the anise seed and mix with flour, sugar, mahleb, and nutmeg in a large bowl, making sure they are blended well. Render the butter. Heat the milk to just warm and add the butter. Sprinkle yeast over the top and let stand for a couple of minutes, until yeast dissolves. Add the liquid to the flour mixture and knead until the dough is smooth and pulls away from the sides of the bowl. Cover with plastic wrap and a towel. Set in a warm place to let rise, about 2 hours.

Nut Filling

Grind walnuts coarsely. Add sugar and orange blossom water. Mix together well.

Syrup

Mix milk and sugar, bring to a boil. Reduce heat and simmer about 5–10 minutes. Keep warm until ready to dip cookies.

Assembly

Divide the dough into thirds, and roll out each to about 1/4 inch thick. Using a doughnut cutter or other utensil, cut into circles about 3 inches in diameter. Put approximately 1 teaspoon filling in the center. Fold the dough over and pinch the edges tightly.

Place the cookies on an ungreased sheet and bake at 400 degrees for 15–20 minutes or until golden brown. Let cool and dip in hot syrup. Place the cookies on racks to dry.

* Can be purchased at Middle Eastern and Greek specialty stores.

SERVINGS: 48

INGREDIENTS
Dough
1/4 cup anise seed
2 1/2 lbs. flour
1 1/2 cups sugar
1/2 teaspoon mahleb*
1/8 teaspoon nutmeg
1 lb. butter
2 cups milk
1 envelope yeast

Nut Filling
1 pound walnuts
1/2 cup sugar
1 tablespoon orange blossom
*   water (Mazahar)**

Syrup
2 cups milk
1 cup sugar

DAILY VALUES

Total Fat	14g
Saturated Fat	5.6g
Cholesterol	23.5mg
Sodium	89mg
Carbohydrate	33g
Dietary Fiber	0.6g
Protein	5.7g

Percent of Daily Values
(2000 Calorie Diet)

Total Fat	18%
Saturated Fat	22%
Cholesterol	8%
Sodium	4%
Carbohydrate	9%
Dietary Fiber	2%
Protein	9%
Calories	275

Easter Cookies

Kaik

SERVINGS: 24

INGREDIENTS
Dough
3/4 cup butter
3 cups milk
1 1/2 cups sugar
1 envelope yeast
1/4 cup anise seed
2 1/2 lbs. flour
1/8 cup mahleb*
1/4 teaspoon nutmeg
1/8 teaspoon salt

Glaze
2 cups sugar
1 quart milk

DAILY VALUES

Total Fat	8.7g
Saturated Fat	5.1g
Cholesterol	25mg
Sodium	105.5mg
Carbohydrate	69.3g
Dietary Fiber	0.3g
Protein	7.7g

*Percent of Daily Values
(2000 Calorie Diet)*

Total Fat	13%
Saturated Fat	25%
Cholesterol	8%
Sodium	4%
Carbohydrate	23%
Dietary Fiber	1%
Protein	15%
Calories	384

Dough
Render the butter and let cool. Warm the milk and add sugar; stir until dissolved and cool to lukewarm. Dissolve yeast in a small amount of the warm milk. Grind the anise seed. Mix flour, mahleb, anise, nutmeg, and salt in a large bowl.

Add butter and yeast to the milk. Gradually add this mixture to the flour, a small amount at a time, working quickly while still warm. Knead together until smooth and the dough no longer sticks to the bowl. Cover and let rest about 2 hours, until dough doubles in size.

Pinch off pieces of the dough and shape into balls about 2 inches in diameter. Let rise again. Keep balls well covered with plastic so the dough does not dry out.

Flatten dough balls and roll out into rounds approximately 1/4 inch thick, flute the edges, and prick the surface with a fork. Cover well and let rest, about 30 minutes. Meanwhile, prepare the glaze.

Place the cookies on an ungreased cookie sheet and bake at 425 degrees for 10–15 minutes, until bottoms are slightly browned. Then place the cookies under the broiler to bring the tops to a golden brown. Watch constantly to prevent burning. Dip the hot cookie into cooled glaze and place on a wire rack to allow the glaze to dry.

Glaze

Add the sugar to the milk and bring to a boil. Reduce heat and simmer for approximately 20 minutes. Let cool.

Note: Test a cookie to see if the inside is doughy; if so, reduce heat and bake a little longer.

* Can be purchased at Middle Eastern and Greek specialty stores.

Above: Fluting the edge of the cookie. Right: Easter cookies on display.

Fritters

Zalabia

SERVINGS: 48

INGREDIENTS
Dough
1 teaspoon anise seed
4 1/2 cups flour
1/2 teaspoon mahleb*
1/4 teaspoon nutmeg (scant)
1 cup milk (scant)
1/3 cup sugar
1 1/2 teaspoons yeast
1 egg
2 1/2 teaspoons oil
2 tablespoons butter
1 ounce beer—optional

Syrup
2 cups water
1 cup sugar
1 teaspoon lemon juice
1 teaspoon orange blossom
  water (Mazahar)*

DAILY VALUES

Total Fat	0.7g
Saturated Fat	0.2g
Cholesterol	5.3mg
Sodium	5.0mg
Carbohydrate	14.8g
Dietary Fiber	0g
Protein	1.6g

Percent of Daily Values
(2000 Calorie Diet)

Total Fat	1%
Saturated Fat	1%
Cholesterol	2%
Sodium	0%
Carbohydrate	4%
Dietary Fiber	0%
Protein	3%

Calories	72

Dough

Grind the anise seed. Put flour in a large bowl and mix in anise, mahleb, and nutmeg. Warm the milk, add sugar and yeast, set aside until yeast dissolves. Beat the egg and add to it the oil. Add the egg to the milk. Gradually pour the liquid into the flour, mixing to incorporate. Add the beer and knead until dough becomes smooth and does not stick to your hands. Cover with plastic wrap, then a towel, and set in a warm place to double in size, about 1 hour.

Syrup

Dissolve sugar in water and bring to a boil. Simmer for approximately 20 minutes. Remove from heat and add the lemon juice and orange blossom water. Set aside to cool.

Assembly

Heat oil (approximately 1 inch deep) in a heavy skillet. Use a little oil or butter on your hands and pinch off pieces of dough about 2 inches in diameter. Stretch and pat them into 2 x 5 inch pieces (about the size of a long john). Poke a hole through the center of each one to ensure even cooking.

Drop the fritters into the hot oil and fry until one side is golden brown; turn and fry the other side. The dough will puff while cooking. Fry only enough at one time to fit comfortably in the skillet. Dip into cooled syrup and drain on cooling rack.

Variation

Sprinkle the fritters with sugar while hot instead
of dipping them into syrup.

* Can be purchased at Middle Eastern and Greek specialty stores.

Rice Pudding

Roz Ib Haleeb

SERVINGS: 6

INGREDIENTS
1/2 cup rice
1 quart milk
1 tablespoon cornstarch
1/2 cup sugar
1 tablespoon orange blossom
  water (Mazahar)*

Rinse and drain the rice. Bring the milk to a boil on medium heat, being careful not to scorch. Add the rice to the milk and cook on low heat for approximately 30 minutes, stirring occasionally.

Mix cornstarch with a little cold water. Add cornstarch and sugar to the rice mixture; cook another 5–10 minutes, until mixture begins to thicken. Add the orange blossom water and cook another minute.

Pour into dessert dishes or custard cups. Let cool to room temperature and refrigerate.

To Serve
Serve chilled and garnish with a dash of cinnamon or crushed pistachio nuts.

* Can be purchased at Middle Eastern and Greek specialty stores.

DAILY VALUES

Total Fat	5.5g
Saturated Fat	3.4g
Cholesterol	22.1mg
Sodium	80.7mg
Carbohydrate	36.6g
Dietary Fiber	0.2g
Protein	6.5g

Percent of Daily Values
(2000 Calorie Diet)

Total Fat	9%
Saturated Fat	17%
Cholesterol	7%
Sodium	3%
Carbohydrate	12%
Dietary Fiber	1%
Protein	13%
Calories	221

Shredded Wheat Cookies

Kannafee

Filling

Grind walnuts, add sugar and orange flower water. Mix well and set aside.

Syrup

Combine sugar and water in saucepan. Cook over low heat until slightly thick, about 20 minutes. Add orange blossom water and lemon juice. Let syrup cool.

Assembly

Heat milk and butter, but do not boil. Quickly dip shredded wheat biscuit in the hot milk. Make an opening in one end of the biscuit and, with a spoon, insert a tablespoon of the filling.

Place the biscuits on a buttered baking sheet and bake at 300 degrees for about 30 minutes, or until golden brown. Remove from oven and pour cooled syrup over the hot kannafee.

* Can be purchased at Middle Eastern and Greek specialty stores.

SERVINGS: 12

INGREDIENTS
Filling
2 cups walnuts
1/2 cup sugar
1 teaspoon orange blossom
  water (Mazahar)*

Syrup
2 cups sugar
1 cup water
1 teaspoon orange blossom
  water
1/2 teaspoon lemon juice

2 cups milk
3 tablespoons butter
1 box Shredded Wheat

DAILY VALUES

Total Fat	16.0g
Saturated Fat	3.4g
Cholesterol	13.2mg
Sodium	50.1mg
Carbohydrate	47.9g
Dietary Fiber	1.3g
Protein	6.7g

Percent of Daily Values
(2000 Calorie Diet)

Total Fat	25%
Saturated Fat	17%
Cholesterol	4%
Sodium	2%
Carbohydrate	16%
Dietary Fiber	5%
Protein	13%
Calories	346

Index

Arabic recipe titles shown in italics.

NOTES

NOTES

NOTES